Teacher's Manual

Building Skills for Social Studies

Virginia Nelson

National Textbook Company
a division of NTC/CONTEMPORARY PUBLISHING GROUP
Lincolnwood, Illinois USA

Acknowledgements

This work is dedicated to the memory of Roe Joseph Nelson and to Jeanne Nelson, Luis Francisco Rivas, Luis José Rivas, and Daniel Rivas.

The author wishes to acknowledge the assistance of Nancy Claussen, Phu Le, Valeria Murga, An Nguyen, Juan Carlos Román, Phuc Tran, and Danny Umaña in the preparation of this series.

ISBN: 0-8442-0516-8
Published by National Textbook Company,
a division of NTC/Contemporary Publishing Group, Inc.
© 1999 NTC/Contemporary Publishing Group, Inc.,
 4255 West Touhy Avenue, Lincolnwood (Chicago), Illinois 60646-1975 U.S.A.

99 00 01 02 03 04 05 06 07 08 09 VP 0 9 8 7 6 5 4 3 2 1

CONTENTS

INTRODUCTION TO THE SERIES

Many students in our intermediate grade, middle school, and high school classrooms need additional literacy skills to perform the more complicated tasks that state standards, guided by school reform, demand. Other students who are learning English need practice to perform at the sophisticated level for which teachers are designing new lessons. All students need an academic challenge.

These skill-building books were written around social studies themes. They provide cross-curricular activities in an accessible format for students who need a content-driven, but not low-level, course of study. They also can serve alongside trade books in whole literacy classrooms in which teachers implement a totally integrated curriculum. The series responds to the need for content-focused, integrated materials with a high graphics/text ratio.

A teacher who works in the classroom, every day, wrote the books for teachers who want to challenge students with a lot of useful work so that they can be fully engaged, active participants in their education. This series of eight books provides that challenge in an accessible format. It leads students to become more efficient at performing the complex tasks and developing the appropriate strategies they will need to achieve academic success.

For students in the general education classroom who are learning English as a second language, *Building Skills* provides a multitude of activities to enhance academic achievement. There are three goals that the TESOL (Teachers of English to Speakers of Other Languages) organization specifies for these students. *Building Skills for Social Studies* addresses each of the three Standards under Goal 2: "To use English to achieve academically in all content areas."

Standard 1 addresses classroom interaction. In each of the eight books in this series, students will interact with and respond to one another and to the teacher. Each point in the "Descriptors" was studied to assure that the objectives of the books and the activities in every lesson match the Standard. "Sample Progress Indicators" were compared to the activities and exercises to make sure that learners are interacting at the level prescribed by the Indicators.

The alignment of curriculum with standards provides a seamless progression of learning for students and a clear directive for teachers. Standard 2 addresses content area learning that students undertake in both written and spoken English. Standard 3, using strategies to apply academic knowledge, requires heavy reliance on study skills, metacognitive strategies, revision and reflection. Again, the Descriptors and the Sample Progress Indicators for both Standards 2 and 3 informed the objectives and the activities in these books.

When deciding which *Building Skills* book to use first, teachers may be guided by topic, by skill, or by the objective(s) they are expected to help students meet. If the objective is to select lessons that match the core social studies curriculum, teachers will note the current topic in the general education classroom and choose a similar topic from the *Building Skills* series.

When a teacher recognizes that most of the students in a class need to improve a skill, that class can move through an entire book. In some classrooms, students need to improve in all of the skills taught in this series. The teacher can order the skills from greatest to least need and begin with the skill that students need most.

In districts where state initiatives govern the curriculum, teachers can begin with the books in the skill areas that most closely match the objectives. In this way, students have the greatest chance to meet prescribed standards.

Although this is an integrated skills series with a social studies focus, each book features a specific skill. The eight skills are: designing charts and graphs, communicating, working with maps, doing math, reading, completing science inquiries, making timelines, and writing.

In this teachers' manual, the author shares with teacher colleagues an introduction to each book and suggests how to use each and provide extension activities to enrich the learning.

CONCLUSION

Building Skills for Social Studies was written by a teacher to serve colleagues who meet classrooms full of students who would approach learning with vigor, were the material accessible. The series is for new and experienced teachers who hold high expectations for every student in their classes. We want all students to enjoy the same educational advantages that the most privileged students enjoy, and we work energetically and relentlessly towards the goal of giving that opportunity to every student in our classrooms.

ABOUT THE AUTHOR

Virginia Nelson has taught ESL students from the university to the elementary level for more than 30 years. She is currently teaching in the Tigard-Tualatin School District in Tigard, Oregon. She has written three previous textbooks, including *Learning to Listen* and *Listen to Communicate* for National Textbook. In addition, Virginia has trained student teachers, presented at numerous conferences such as NSTA (National Science Teachers Association) and TESOL, and was the 1999 Oregon Intel Innovations in Teaching Award Winner.

BUILDING CHARTING AND GRAPHING SKILLS FOR SOCIAL STUDIES

Introduction

Charts are graphic organizers. In their various formats, they arrange information and synthesize facts. Their value lies in the way they allow readers to see a lot of information plotted concisely in a single representation. Even students who lack strong language skills can develop and interpret graphs and tables.

Building Charting and Graphing Skills for Social Studies assists students by introducing metacognitive strategies for accessing content area text. All the exercises in the book respect the heightened emphasis on graphic organizers as tools to develop metacognition and strengthen cognitive skills. Students must be efficient chart readers. More than that, they must be able to create charts from information. Some of the performance tasks that we are seeing in statewide assessments call for a chart as partial evidence in the development of an answer.

Beyond understanding and designing charts, students can expect to have to interpret them for others. This book includes activities through which students learn to ask and answer questions about charts. They also must describe the charted information in paragraphs and short oral presentations. By connecting each lesson to a social studies topic, the exercises introduce content as they prepare students to master the skills.

HOW TO USE THIS BOOK

Odd-numbered lessons contain these sections:

Get Ready

This prereading section activates prior knowledge and brings learners to the topic of the lesson.

Read a Graph

In this section students study a complete graph. Several types of graphs appear. They include bar, line, scatter, and pie graphs.

Answer the Questions

In this activity, students find facts in the graph in response to questions. The activity introduces different ways to ask a question, giving students the guidance they need to begin to formulate different questions.

Describe a Graph

Reading facts accurately from graphed information enables learners to absorb a lot of information quickly. This introduction to interpreting graphed data orally and in writing helps learners expand the graphed information. They demonstrate that they comprehend the context of the discreet facts as they pull them from the graph.

Make a Table

In this exercise, learners organize the graphed information to make it accessible in a different format. They convert data from graphic to tabular form. Tabulating information is an important synthesis exercise because it permits learners to reduce a large volume of text to an easy to understand list of facts.

Fun Fact

This is an amusing or interesting fact about the lesson topic.

Complete the Paragraph

In this concluding activity students complete a paragraph that is similar to the written proofs students must prepare for open-ended problems on the state assessments. As students develop a statement to answer a question from graphed and tabulated data, they practice sequential narrative writing. The activity guides students as they supply facts from graph and table. Finally they review the lesson by reading their paragraphs to one another.

Make a Connection
This activity helps learners connect the lesson to other areas of the curriculum. Like the Extension Activities in this Teacher's Manual, this activity broadens the lesson topic.

<u>Even numbered lessons contain these sections:</u>

Get Ready
This prereading section activates prior knowledge and brings learners to the topic of the lesson.

Collect the Data
Students scan text for data, preparing to develop a graph. Grade-level books overwhelm many students. An important metacognitive strategy that helps these students is to look for words in italic or bold print. By highlighting these words in the text, they reduce the material, making it less formidable to study and learn.

Fun Fact
This is an amusing or interesting fact about the lesson topic.

Make a Table
With the data highlighted, students synthesize the information. Many texts ask students to read tables, but they seldom ask them to create a table. By learning how tables are made, students find it easier to interpret them.

Describe a Table
In this activity students relate tabulated data orally. Assign the description only after the table is complete and accurate.

Make a Graph
Although we expect students to interpret graphs in almost every area of the curriculum, many students lack practice in developing and designing graphs. Converting text into a graphic representation requires planning. It often requires several repetitions. Each graph is set up, and each contains some data. First students will plan how to complete the graph. Next they will complete it in their notebooks, check it with a classmate or you, and finally transfer it to the book. Or, they can pencil it lightly in the book, check it, and then complete it with ink, markers, or crayons.

Read a Graph
Asking questions is the basis of inquiry learning. Students are expected to be able to ask questions now as much as they are expected to answer them. In fact, on some college applications there is now an essay question for which students must ask a question, then answer it! To practice locating data on the graph in the preceding exercise, students will formulate questions from the graph. Some students will be able to complete this section orally. However, all students should prepare their questions in writing because the activity provides an individual summary of the lesson content.

Make a Connection
This activity helps learners connect the lesson to other areas of the curriculum. Like the Extension Activities in this Teacher's Manual, it broadens the lesson topic.

EXTENSION ACTIVITIES

Get Ready
Teachers and learners can expand this section in each lesson to match the language competence of the class. Some activities for learners:

- Introduce photos or realia connected to a lesson, such as photos of the presidents (Lessons 1 and 2—20th Century Presidents) or toy cars (Lesson 7—Cars: A Big Production).

- Copy questions from the book and answers from the board.

- Read and answer questions in pairs.

- In groups, write additional questions.

- Research the topic before completing the lesson.

Fun Fact

Teachers might introduce additional fun facts for each lesson. Some activities for learners:

- Create a different illustration for the fun fact.

- Write and illustrate a fun fact about the class.

- Find a chart or a graph in another textbook and design a fun fact from the data.

- Search for additional facts about the lesson topic in encyclopedias or on the Internet.

- Locate fun facts in the community. These could be data on topics such as ridership on the local bus line, local newspaper circulation, average daily absenteeism at school, or the number of students who walk to school.

Make a Connection

This section activity provides an in-book extension activity for each lesson.

EXTENSION ACTIVITIES FOR ODD-NUMBERED LESSONS

Read a Graph

In this section, students at different levels will be able to do different activities with the graph. Some activities for learners:

- Copy the graph.

- Point to parts of the graph as someone names them, or name parts of the graph as someone points to them.

- Ask and/or answer questions about the graph.

- Discuss the graph in pairs.

Answer the Questions

Some activities for learners:

- Copy questions from the book and answers from the board.

- Listen to the questions while looking at the graph.

- Answer the questions by listening to them.

- In pairs, ask and answer questions.

Describe a Graph

Some activities for learners:

- Locate graphs in other textbooks and describe them orally and in writing.

- Using the same graphs, write questions about them for classmates to answer.

- Elaborate on the answer examples in the book, giving additional information.

- Describe a simple graph to the class, one that the class cannot see. The classmates attempt to draw it from the description.

Make a Table
Some activities for learners:

- Transform horizontal tables to vertical tables, and vice versa.

- Use different symbols to represent items in the table.

- Make tables of different data from the class, such as shirt colors, weather preferences or languages spoken.

- Design a table to synthesize some data and explain it to a partner, group, or the class.

Complete the Paragraph
Some activities for learners:

- Copy the entire paragraph from the book to a notebook for additional practice.

- Rewrite a paragraph from a textbook, omit words, and develop a new "Complete the Paragraph" to share with classmates.

- Find graphs in other textbooks and write brief descriptions of them.

- Borrow a book on tape from an organization that serves visually impaired learners and listen to a description of a graph. Repeat the description and write it in a notebook.

EXTENSION ACTIVITIES FOR EVEN-NUMBERED LESSONS

Collect the Data
Some activities for learners to work on metacognitive strategies for attacking grade-level text:

- Highlight italicized and boldfaced words in a photocopied page from another textbook.

- Predict what happens in a chapter by looking at the illustrations.

- After looking at illustrations and reading captions, suggest what the topic of a chapter might be.

- Write a paragraph with students' names and birth dates, then highlight the surnames and dates in the paragraph.

Make a Table
Some activities for learners to practice organizing facts:

- Design a table about family and share it.

- In groups, make a table about something in the class.

- Tabulate lunch menu choices and other school information.

- Reorganize tables from horizontal to vertical, and vice versa.

Describe a Table
Some activities for learners:

- Copy sentences from the text and read them aloud.

- Experiment with syntax by changing the sentences from the passage.

- Write sentences for other students to read aloud.

Make a Graph
Some activities for learners:

- Graph data from the class, such as food preferences.

- Graph weather data for the week.

- Change a bar graph to a pictogram.

- Enlarge a graph from the lesson to post on a wall.

Read a Graph
Some activities for learners:

- Review the material with a partner by asking and answering questions.

- Read the questions and the answers.

- Say an answer without reading it.

- Ask and answer questions without referring to the written questions.

ANSWER KEY, BUILDING CHARTING AND GRAPHING SKILLS

Answers are given where they are definitive. In many instances answers will vary. The integrated feature of the series means students will derive unique answers depending on how they respond to the questions.

LESSON 1: 20TH-CENTURY PRESIDENTS

A. Get Ready (Page 1)
Some presidents have died in office. One resigned.

C. Answer the Questions (Page 2)
1. McKinley served as president for four and a half years.
2. Wilson served as president for eight years.
3. Coolidge served as president for five and a half years.
4. Hoover served as president for four years.
5. Franklin D. Roosevelt served as president for 12 years.

D. Describe a Graph (Page 2)
Students' descriptive sentences will vary depending on the presidents they choose. (President's name) was president for ____ years.

E. Make a Table (Page 3)

President	Number of Years Served
William McKinley	4 1/2
Theodore Roosevelt	7 1/2
William H. Taft	4
Woodrow Wilson	8
Warren G. Harding	2 1/2
Calvin Coolidge	5 1/2
Herbert C. Hoover	4
Franklin D. Roosevelt	12
Harry S Truman	8

Served 4 Years	William H. Taft Herbert C. Hoover
Served 8 Years	Woodrow Wilson Harry S Truman
Served 12 Years	Franklin D. Roosevelt
Other Presidents	William McKinley Theodore Roosevelt Warren G. Harding Calvin Coolidge

F. Complete the Paragraph (Page 4)
First, I see that <u>two</u> presidents served for four years. They were <u>William H. Taft</u> and <u>Herbert C. Hoover.</u> Next, I see that <u>two</u> presidents served for eight years. They were <u>Woodrow Wilson</u> and <u>Harry S Truman.</u> One president served for 12 years. He was <u>Franklin D. Roosevelt.</u> One president served less than four years. He was <u>Warren G. Harding.</u> William McKinley served <u>four and a half years;</u> Theodore Roosevelt, <u>seven and a half;</u> and Calvin Coolidge, <u>five and a half.</u>

G. Make a Connection (Page 4)
1. Virginia—Woodrow Wilson
2. Vermont—Calvin Coolidge
3. Iowa—Herbert C. Hoover
4. Missouri—Harry S Truman
5. New York—Theodore Roosevelt and Franklin D. Roosevelt
6. Ohio—William McKinley, William H. Taft, and Warren G. Harding

LESSON 2: MORE 20TH-CENTURY PRESIDENTS

A. Get Ready (Page 5)
1. Answers will vary depending on the year.
2. Answers will vary according to where students live.

B. Collect the Data (Page 5)
The next nine presidents served from two and a half years to eight years. <u>Dwight D. Eisenhower</u> was in office for <u>eight</u> years. <u>John F. Kennedy</u> was president for <u>three</u> years. <u>Lyndon B. Johnson</u> served for <u>five</u> years. <u>Richard M. Nixon</u> had the job for <u>five and a half</u> years.

Gerald R. Ford served for two and a half years. James E. Carter was in office for four years. After Carter came Ronald Reagan, who served eight years. Then George Bush was president for four years. William (Bill) J. Clinton took office in 1993. How long did he serve?

C. Make a Table (Page 6)

President	Number of Years Served
Dwight D. Eisenhower	8
John F. Kennedy	3
Lyndon B. Johnson	5
Richard M. Nixon	5 1/2
Gerald R. Ford	2 1/2
James E. Carter	4
Ronald Reagan	8
George Bush	4
William J. Clinton	Answers will vary. (His second term ends in 2000)

D. Describe a Table (Page 6)
Students' descriptive sentences will vary depending on the presidents they choose.

E. Make a Graph (Page 7)

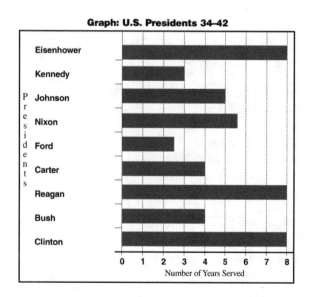

Graph: U.S. Presidents 34–42

Presidents: Eisenhower, Kennedy, Johnson, Nixon, Ford, Carter, Reagan, Bush, Clinton

Number of Years Served

F. Read a Graph (Page 7)
Students' questions and answers will vary depending on the presidents they choose.

G. Make a Connection (Page 8)
1. California—Richard M. Nixon
2. Nebraska—Gerald R. Ford
3. Georgia—James E. Carter
4. Illinois—Ronald Reagan
5. Arkansas—William J. Clinton
6. Texas—Dwight D. Eisenhower and Lyndon B. Johnson
7. Massachusetts—John F. Kennedy and George Bush

LESSON 3: REPRESENTING THE PEOPLE

C. Answer the Questions (Page 10)
1. Maine sends two.
2. Eight representatives go to Congress from Minnesota.
3. Louisiana has seven representatives.
4. Kentucky has six representatives in Congress.
5. Massachusetts sends ten.

D. Describe a Graph (Page 10)
Students' descriptive sentences will vary depending on the states they choose.

E. Make a Table (Page 11)

State	Postal Abbreviation	Number of Representatives
Iowa	IA	5
Kansas	KS	4
Kentucky	KY	6
Louisiana	LA	7
Maine	ME	2
Maryland	MD	8
Massachusetts	MA	10
Minnesota	MN	8

F. Complete the Paragraph (Page 12)
First I studied the graph and the table. I can see that Iowa has five representatives. Kansas sends four. Six go from Kentucky. Louisiana has seven. Voters from Maine send two representatives to Washington, D.C. Eight go to the House of Representatives from Maryland. Massachusetts sends ten. Voters in Minnesota have eight representatives.

G. Make a Connection (Page 12)

1. KY–6
2. LA–7
3. KS–4
4. MN–8
5. ME–2
6. MA–10
7. IA–5
8. MD–8

LESSON 4: COMING TO AMERICA

A. Get Ready (Page 13)

1. An **immigrant** is a person who has moved to a new country.
2. Answers will vary to both questions.

B. Collect the Data (Page 13)

People immigrate (move into a country) for many reasons. Sometimes they leave problems in their home countries. Sometimes they need jobs. Some immigrants want to join their families.

From 1991 to 1996 more than six million people immigrated to the United States. The <u>total</u> number was <u>6,146,213.</u> <u>Europe</u> was the homeland for <u>916,733</u> of them. For <u>1,875,391,</u> <u>Asia</u> was the homeland. There were <u>3,119,506</u> immigrants from the <u>Americas.</u> There were <u>198,068</u> immigrants from <u>Africa.</u> The other <u>36,515</u> immigrants came from <u>other countries.</u>

C. Make a Table (Page 14)

Homeland	Number of Immigrants
Europe	916,733
Asia	1,875,391
The Americas	3,119,506
Africa	198,068
Other Countries	36,515
Total	6,146,213

D. Describe a Table (Page 14)

Students' descriptive sentences will vary.

E. Make a Graph (Page 15)

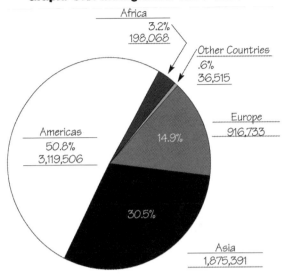

Graph: U.S. Immigration 1991–1996

Africa
3.2%
198,068

Other Countries
.6%
36,515

Europe
916,733

14.9%

Americas
50.8%
3,119,506

30.5%

Asia
1,875,391

F. Read a Graph (Page 15)

Students' questions and answers will vary depending on the countries and figures they choose.

G. Make a Connection (Page 16)

1. The Americas—3,119,506
2. Africa—198,068
3. Asia—1,875,391
4. Europe—916,733

LESSON 5: HOME, SWEET HOME

A. Get Ready (Page 17)

Answers will vary for each student.

C. Answer the Questions (Page 18)

1. 23 million
2. five
3. 14.5 million
4. seven or more
5. 30.1 million

D. Describe a Graph (Page 18)

Students' sentences will vary depending on the data they choose.

E. Make a Table (Page 19)

People in Household	Number of Households
1	23 million
2	30.1 million
3	16.1 million
4	14.5 million
5	6.2 million
6	2.1 million
7 or more	1.3 million

F. Complete the Paragraph (Page 20)

To answer this question, I looked at the graph and the table. I see that <u>23 million</u> households had <u>one</u> person. In <u>30.1 million</u> households there were <u>two</u> people. About <u>16.1 million</u> households had <u>three</u> people. There were <u>four</u> people in each of <u>14.5 million</u> households. In <u>6.2 million</u> households there were <u>five</u> people. The number of households with <u>six</u> people was <u>2.1 million</u>. Finally, <u>seven</u> or more people lived in each of <u>1.3 million</u> households.

G. Make a Connection (Page 20)

Students' charts will vary based on the makeup of the class.

LESSON 6: TALK, TALK, TALK

A. Get Ready (Page 21)

Answers will vary for both questions.

B. Collect the Data (Page 21)

People speak many languages in the United States. One language is <u>Chinese.</u> In 1990 about <u>1,249,000</u> U.S. residents spoke Chinese at home. About <u>1,702,000</u> spoke <u>French</u> at home. Around <u>1,547,000</u> people spoke <u>German,</u> and approximately <u>1,309,000</u> people spoke <u>Italian.</u> About <u>626,000</u> people spoke <u>Korean,</u> and around <u>723,000</u> spoke <u>Polish.</u> There were approximately <u>17,339,000</u> <u>Spanish</u> speakers, <u>843,000</u> <u>Tagalog</u> speakers, and <u>507,000</u> <u>Vietnamese</u> speakers. About <u>198,601,000</u> U.S. residents spoke only <u>English</u> at home that year.

C. Make a Table (Page 22)

Language	Number of Speakers
Chinese	1,249,000
French	1,702,000
German	1,547,000
Italian	1,309,000
Korean	626,000
Polish	723,000
Spanish	17,339,000
Tagalog	843,000
Vietnamese	507,000

D. Describe a Table (Page 22)

Students' sentences will vary according to the countries they choose.

E. Make a Graph (Page 23)

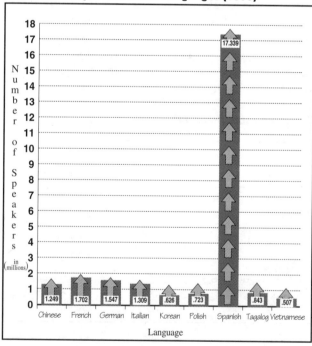

Graph: U.S. Home Languages (1990)

F. Read a Graph (Page 24)

Students' questions and answers will vary according to the countries they choose.

G. Make a Connection (Page 24)

The contents of students' tables will vary according to the population of the classroom.

LESSON 7: CARS: A BIG PRODUCTION

B. Read a Graph (Page 25)
Explain that the graph is two separate graphs divided by a vertical line. The graph on the left goes from zero to 180,000 cars and provides data for the years 1900 and 1910. The graph on the right goes from zero to 9,000,000 cars and provides data for the years 1920 and 1950.

C. Answer the Questions (Page 26)
1. 1900
2. 1910
3. 1920
4. 1950
5. Answers will vary, but it is reasonable to expect that guesses for 1930 will be more than 2,227,000 and less than 8,003,056 and that guesses for 1940 will be more than those for 1930 and less than 8,003,056.

D. Describe a Graph (Page 26)
Students' sentences will vary according to the data they select.

E. Make a Table (Page 27)

Year	Number of Vehicles Produced
1900	4,192
1910	180,000
1920	2,227,000
1950	8,003,056

F. Complete the Paragraph (Page 28)
Were more vehicles produced in 1950 or in 1900, 1910, and 1920 together?

To answer this question, I looked at the graph and the table. I can see that 8,003,056 vehicles were produced in the United States in 1950. In 1900, 4,192 vehicles were produced. In 1910, 180,000 vehicles were made. In 1920, 2,227,000 vehicles were made. I added the totals for those three years: 4,192 plus 180,000 plus 2,227,000 equals 2,411,192. 8,003,056 is greater than 2,411,192. Therefore, more vehicles were made in the United States in 1950 than in 1900,1910, and 1920 together.

G. Make a Connection (Page 28)
Students' tables will vary according to the data they gather.

LESSON 8: WHO'S WATCHING TV?

B. Collect the Data (Page 29)
Scientists from Germany, Russia, Scotland, and the United States worked to invent television. These television experiments started in the 1880s. They continued into the 1920s and 1930s.

In 1936 there were about 150 TVs in U.S. homes. During World War II, television work slowed. After that, TV production grew quickly. In 1945 there were about 10,000 TVs in U.S. homes. In 1950 there were about 6,000,000 TVs in U.S. homes. There were almost 60,000,000 TVs in U.S. homes in 1960.

C. Make a Table (Page 30)

Year	Number of TVs
1936	150
1945	10,000
1950	6,000,000
1960	60,000,000

D. Describe a Table
Students' sentences will vary according to the data they choose.

E. Make a Graph (Page 31)

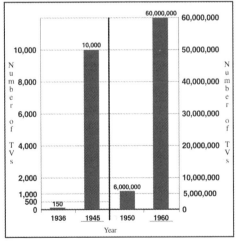

Graph: Number of TVs in U.S. Homes

F. Read a Graph (Page 32)
Students' questions and answers will vary according to the data they choose.

G. Make a Connection (Page 32)
Students' tables will vary according to the data they gather from newspapers.

LESSON 9: GLOBAL WARMING: A HOT TOPIC

C. Answer the Questions (Page 34)
1. It could be 0.6 degrees hotter.
2. It could be 1 degree hotter.
3. It could be 0.75 degrees hotter.
4. It could be 1.5 degrees hotter.
5. It could be 3 degrees hotter.

D. Describe a Graph (Page 34)
Students' sentences will vary according to the data they select from the graph.

E. Make a Table (Page 35)

Year	0.15°F Increase	0.5°F Increase
1990	0	0
2000	0.15°F	0.5°F
2010	0.30°F	1°F
2020	0.45°F	1.5°F
2030	0.6°F	2°F
2040	0.75°F	2.5°F
2050	0.9°F	3°F

F. Complete the Paragraph (Page 36)
Compare temperatures in 2050. What will the temperature be in 2050 if there is no global warming? What could it be if the temperature rises 0.15°F each decade? If it rises 0.5°F each decade?

First I studied the graph and the table. If there is no global warming, the temperature will be the same in 2050 as in 1990. If the temperature rises 0.15° F each decade, it could be 0.9° F warmer in 2050 than in 1990. If the temperature rises 0.5° F each decade, it could be 3° F warmer in 2050 than in 1990.

G. Make a Connection (Page 36)
Students' results will differ depending on variables applied to the experiment—for example, the source of heat, the amount of water used, and the type of container used to hold the water. Students might enjoy repeating the experiment, keeping the variables the same, to see if they come out with the same results, or they might repeat the experiment, changing one of the variables, to see if the results differ.

LESSON 10: WHAT TIME IS IT?

A. Get Ready (Page 37)
1. Answers will vary.
2. No. Students often know that; however, some are not aware of it.

B. Collect the Data (Page 37)
Each day the earth turns one time. Each day has 24 hours. There are 24 time zones. The time is later to the east. It is earlier to the west.

These are the U.S. time zones: Eastern, Central, Mountain, Pacific, Alaska, and Hawaii-Aleutian. Some North American cities in the Eastern time zone are New York, NY; Washington, DC; Baltimore, MD; Jacksonville, FL; and Ottawa and Montreal, Canada. These cities are in the Central time zone: Chicago, IL; St. Louis and Kansas City, MO; Dallas, TX; New Orleans, LA; Mexico City, Mexico; and Winnipeg, Canada.

Cities in the Mountain time zone include Helena, MT; Denver, CO; Phoenix, AZ; and Edmonton, Canada. Seattle, WA; San Francisco and Los Angeles, CA; and Vancouver, Canada, are in the Pacific time zone. Two cities in the Alaska time zone are Nome and Anchorage, AK. Honolulu, HI, is in the Hawaii-Aleutian time zone.

C. Make a Table (Page 38)

Eastern	Central	Mountain
New York, NY	Chicago, IL	Helena, MT
Washington, DC	St. Louis, MO	Denver, CO
Baltimore, MD	Kansas City, MO	Phoenix, AZ
Jacksonville, FL	Dallas, TX	Edmonton, Canada
Ottawa, Canada	New Orleans, LA	
Montreal, Canada	Mexico City, Mexico	
	Winnipeg, Canada	

Pacific	Alaska	Hawaii-Aleutian
Seattle, WA	Nome, AK	Honolulu, HI
San Francisco	Anchorage, AK	
Los Angeles, CA		
Vancouver, Canada		

D. Describe a Table (Page 38)
Students' sentences will vary according to the cities they choose.

E. Make a Graph (Page 39)

Graph: Cities and Their Time Zones

City	Hawaii-Aleutian	Alaska	Pacific	Mountain	Central	Eastern
Anchorage, AK		X				
Baltimore, MD						X
Chicago, IL					X	
Dallas, TX					X	
Denver, CO				X		
Edmonton, Canada				X		
Helena, MT				X		
Honolulu, HI	X					
Jacksonville, FL						X
Kansas City, MO					X	
Los Angeles, CA			X			
Mexico City, Mexico					X	
Montreal, Canada					'	X
New Orleans, LA					X	
New York, NY						X
Nome, AK		X				
Ottawa, Canada						X
Phoenix, AZ				X		
San Francisco, CA			X			
Seattle, WA			X			
St. Louis, MO					X	
Vancouver, Canada			X			
Washington, DC						X
Winnipeg, Canada					X	

Time Zone

F. Read a Graph (Page 40)
Students' sentences will vary according to their choices of time zones and cities.

G. Make A Connection

LESSON 11: THE GREAT LAKES

C. Answer the Questions (Page 42)
1. It is 350 miles long.
2. It is 53 miles wide.
3. It is 307 miles long.
4. It is 183 miles wide.
5. It is 241 miles long.
6. Lake Huron is the widest.
7. Lake Superior is the longest.

D. Describe a Graph (Page 42)
Students' sentences will vary according to the lakes and data they choose.

E. Make a Table (Page 43)

Lake	Length	Breadth
Huron	206	183
Ontario	193	53
Michigan	307	118
Erie	241	57
Superior	350	160

F. Complete the Paragraph (Page 44)
What is the difference in length between the longest lake and the shortest lake?

First we need to know which lake is the longest. We need to know which lake is the shortest. Lake Huron is 206 miles long. Lake <u>Ontario</u> is <u>193</u>

miles long. <u>Lake Michigan</u> is <u>307</u> miles long. <u>Lake Erie</u> is <u>241</u> miles long. <u>Lake Superior</u> is <u>350</u> miles long. Therefore, Lake <u>Superior</u> is the longest lake. Lake <u>Ontario</u> is the shortest lake. To find the difference, I subtracted: <u>350</u> miles minus <u>193</u> miles equals <u>157</u> miles.

Lake <u>Superior</u> is longer than Lake <u>Ontario</u> by <u>157</u> miles.

G. Make a Connection (Page 44)

LESSON 12: RIVERS OF THE AMERICAS

A. Get Ready (Page 45)
Answers for both questions will vary.

B. Collect the Data (Page 45)
The longest river in the Americas is the <u>Amazon</u> in South America. It is almost <u>4,000</u> miles long. Other rivers in South America are the <u>Japurá</u>, about <u>1,750</u> miles long; the <u>Madeira</u>, about <u>2,000</u> miles long; the <u>Paraná</u>, about <u>2,450</u>; the <u>Purus</u>, about <u>1,995</u>; and the <u>São Francisco</u>, about <u>1,800</u>.

The <u>Mackenzie River</u> in Canada is about <u>1,070</u> miles long. The <u>Missouri River</u> in the United States is about <u>2,540</u> miles long. Other U.S. rivers are the <u>Mississippi</u>, about <u>2,340</u> miles long, and the <u>Ohio</u>, about <u>980</u> miles long. The <u>Río Grande</u>, between the United States and Mexico, is about <u>1,885</u> miles long. The <u>Yukon</u>, in Alaska and Canada, is about <u>1,979</u> miles long.

C. Make a Table (Page 46)

River	Location	Approximate Length
Amazon	South America	4,000 miles
Japurá	South America	1,750 miles
Madeira	South America	2,000 miles
Paraná	South America	2,450 miles
Purus	South America	1,995 miles
São Francisco	South America	1,800 miles
Mackenzie	Canada	1,070 miles
Missouri	United States	2,540 miles
Mississippi	United States	2,340 miles
Ohio	United States	980 miles
Rio Grande	United States and Mexico	1,885 miles
Yukon	Alaska (U.S.) and Canada	1,979 miles

D. Describe a Table (Page 46)
Students' sentences will vary according to the rivers they choose.

E. Make a Graph (Page 47)
The completed graph should have the names of the rivers filled in the blank spaces. The order of rivers from the top of the graph to the bottom is
Amazon
Japurá
Mackenzie
Madeira
Mississippi
Missouri
Ohio
Paraná
Purus
Rio Grande
São Francisco
Yukon

F. Read a Graph (Page 48)
Students' questions and answers will vary according to the rivers they choose.

LESSON 13: WETLANDS: THE BIG SPONGES

C. Answer the Questions (Page 50)
1. Alabama, Colorado, and Michigan have.
2. Texas, Tennessee, Pennsylvania, New York, Nevada, Mississippi, Idaho, and Delaware have.

3. Maryland, Connecticut, and Arkansas have.
4. Ohio, Missouri, Iowa, Indiana, Illinois, and California have.
5. California has lost the most.

D. Describe a Graph (Page 50)
Students' sentences will vary according to the states they choose.

E. Make a Table (Page 51)

State	Postal Abbreviation	Wetlands Lost
Alabama	AL	50%
Arkansas	AR	72%
California	CA	91%
Colorado	CO	50%
Connecticut	CT	74%
Delaware	DE	54%
Idaho	ID	56%
Illinois	IL	85%
Indiana	IN	87%
Iowa	IA	89%
Kentucky	KY	81%
Maryland	MD	74%
Michigan	MI	50%
Mississippi	MS	59%
Missouri	MO	87%
Nevada	NV	52%
New York	NY	60%
Ohio	OH	90%
Oklahoma	OK	67%
Pennsylvania	PA	56%
Tennessee	TN	59%
Texas	TX	52%

F. Complete the Paragraph (Page 52)
What is the difference between the largest and smallest percentages of wetlands lost?

First I looked at the graph and the table. I see that 50% is the smallest loss. The states with 50% wetland loss are Michigan, Colorado, and Alabama. The state with the largest wetland loss is California. Its loss is 91%. Next I subtracted the smallest loss from the largest loss: 91% minus 50% equals 41%. This is the difference between the largest loss and the smallest loss.

G. Make a Connection (Page 52)
1. The loss of water should be negligible and may not even be measurable.

2. Students' answers will vary depending on the size and absorbency of the sponge used in the experiment.

LESSON 14: NEIGHBOR TO THE NORTH: CANADA

A. Get Ready (Page 53)
Answers will vary.

B. Collect the Data (Page 53)
Canada is the United States's neighbor to the north. Canada is a very big country. It has a small population. More people live in California than in all of Canada!

In 1996 Canada had 10 **provinces** and two **territories**. About 31,000 people lived in the Yukon Territory. About 64,400 lived in the Northwest Territories.

The province of Alberta had almost 2,700,000 people in 1996. British Columbia had nearly 3,725,000. There were about 1,114,000 in Manitoba. New Brunswick had about 738,000, and Newfoundland had about 552,000. There were about 909,000 people in Nova Scotia. Ontario had about 10,754,000, but Prince Edward Island had only about 135,000. Quebec had about 7,139,000 people, and Saskatchewan had about 990,000.

Province/Territory	Approximate Population
Yukon Territory	31,000
Northwest Territories	64,400
Alberta	2,700,000
British Columbia	3,725,000
Manitoba	1,114,000
New Brunswick	738,000
Newfoundland	552,000
Nova Scotia	909,000
Ontario	10,754,000
Prince Edward Island	135,000
Quebec	7,139,000
Saskatchewan	990,000

C. Make a Table (Page 54)

D. Describe a Table (Page 54)
Students' sentences will vary according to the provinces or territories they choose.

E. Make a Graph (Page 55)

Graph: The Population of Canada (1996)

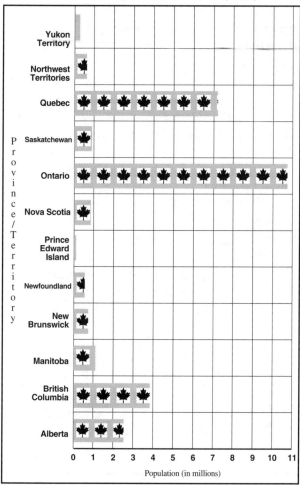

Population (in millions)

F. Read a Graph (Page 56)

Students' questions and answers will vary according to the provinces or territories they choose.

G. Make a Connection (Page 56)

LESSON 15: NEIGHBOR TO THE SOUTH: MEXICO

C. Answer the Questions (Page 58)

1. 11%
2. 11%
3. 17%
4. services
5. mining

D. Describe a Graph (Page 58)

Students' sentences will vary according to the data they choose.

E. Make a Table (Page 59)

Type of Work	Workers
Services	29%
Agriculture	26%
Trade	15%
Construction	11%
Manufacturing	11%
Transportation and Communication	5%
Finance	2%
Mining	1%

F. Complete the Paragraph (Page 60)

In 1991 did more Mexican people work in services and agriculture or in all other jobs combined?

First I looked at the graph and the table. I see that <u>29%</u> of the jobs were in services. <u>26%</u> of the jobs were in agriculture. Then I added those numbers: <u>29%</u> plus <u>26%</u> equals <u>55%.</u>

Next I found the percentages of workers in other jobs. There were 15% in <u>trade</u> jobs and 5% in <u>transportation and communication.</u> Manufacturing and construction each had <u>11%</u> of the workers.

<u>Finance</u> had 2% of the workers. The last <u>1%</u> worked in <u>mining.</u> Then I added those numbers: <u>15%</u> plus <u>5%</u> plus <u>11%</u> plus <u>11%</u> plus <u>2%</u> plus <u>1%</u> equals <u>45%.</u>

In 1991 the percentage of Mexican workers in services and agriculture was <u>more than</u> the percentage of workers in all other jobs.

G. Make a Connection (Page 60)

Spanish	English
agricultura	agriculture
comunicación	communication
construcción	construction
servicios	services
transporte	transportation

BUILDING COMMUNICATION SKILLS FOR SOCIAL STUDIES

INTRODUCTION

Building Communication Skills for Social Studies integrates fifteen social studies topics with communication activities. The learner practices formal and informal speaking, writing, and reading. This book includes opportunities to develop oral fluency in reading, as well as other communication activities. Exercises on highlighting and underlining help students learn and practice study skills, too.

Speaking is the greatest risk-taking communication skill. We want students to speak out because Americans place great value on oral expression. Many Americans abhor silence and do not see it as a form of communication. We have many English Language Learners (ELLs) in our classrooms. For these students, speaking out can be a terrifying experience. We must take a long-term view: Do we want these students to speak in class right away, however poorly, and at whatever cost to their confidence? Or, will we wait two years for the more reluctant speakers to begin to express themselves with more comfort and ease? Patience produces a better speaker.

In some schools ELLs who do not speak any English after a year are tested for inclusion in special education. This inappropriate practice comes from the research finding that the *average* "silent period" can last one year. This is the time during which the newcomer is acquiring enough language to want to speak it. The one year is an average, however. Some students need more time.

Once students are willing to speak, teachers can ask questions and offer alternative answers.

Example:

Was Bill Clinton president in the 1980s or the 1990s?

Who was president in the 1990s, Bill Clinton or Abraham Lincoln?

This is the progression of stages in a newcomer's willingness to speak out in the classroom:

1. To a teacher or friend

2. To two or three supportive classmates

3. To a larger group

4. To the whole class

HOW TO USE THIS BOOK

The goal of *Building Communication Skills* is for students to use paraphrasing and memorizing to improve their communication skills. The best way to learn how to compose correct and articulate statements is to practice doing so. Paraphrasing and memorization are essential activities for someone who is beginning to improve their communication skills. The goal of this book, though, is not for students to paraphrase and memorize. It is for them to employ paraphrasing and memorization as they learn to improve their communication skills.

By working in groups, in pairs, and as individuals, students try out a variety of communication techniques. These include study skills such as scanning text and synthesizing information. They learn to formulate questions and exchange information. Speaking out is risk-taking. In this book students develop the skills that will give them the confidence to take that risk.

The text alternates between two lesson formats, though all fifteen lessons begin with the same introductory exercises.

ACTIVITIES FOR ALL LESSONS

Preview

The **Preview** instructs students to look at the illustration. Two **Focus Questions** suggest how teachers can ask about the illustration, and help complete these tasks:

- Activate prior knowledge

- Assess individual learners' schema

- Judge students' interest in and enthusiasm for the topic

- Provide opportunities for students to make predictions and support them with evidence

- Offer a risk-free learning environment in which casual, structured conversation can take place.

Under each lesson heading there are suggestions for different types of questions. Select the questions that match students' language abilities. Our classrooms serve learners with varying language skills. Therefore, you might select a "Point to . . . " activity and a "Make a prediction . . ." activity.

Reading

In this section, students prepare to complete the exercises in the lesson. To start the reading, you or a competent reader in the class may read the passage. If you are not a native speaker, you may wish to play the reading on the audiocassette. Use a tape recorder with a meter, and rewind the tape to the beginning after completing the reading.

Students with developing skills should follow the written words by pointing to them with a finger or a pencil. The stronger students will move the pointer in a smooth, uninterrupted line across the page. The other students will lift the pointer and set it down under each word. Noting this pointing practice allows you to roughly gauge the level of exposure to reading among beginning readers. Model reading behaviors as you encourage students to move from one level to another.

More skillful learners can set a bookmark under each line as it is read. The experienced readers will follow without any assistance from pointers or bookmarks.

Vocabulary

Words are listed in the **Vocabulary** box in the order in which they occur in the reading. The instructor pronounces each word, and students repeat the word up to five times. Clapping the syllables or chanting the words assists some learners in remembering stress patterns.

In cooperative groups, students can give themselves a number "1" to "4." Call a number. All students assigned that number rise and repeat a word five times. One way to decide which number to call is by numbering tongue depressors and placing them number-side down in a can. After you or a student remove and call one of the numbers, replace it in the can. This technique will keep all students ready for their next turn.

Another way to select students for this exercise is to use a spinner. A student can spin a large vertical spinner mounted on a wall. A plastic opaque spinner set on an overhead projector can also be used. The spinner can look like this:

Who's next?

Students then circle or highlight the vocabulary in the passage. Some learners will want to keep vocabulary lists in their notebooks. Others might want to make flashcards.

Students whose primary language (L_1) is not English should be able to discuss the vocabulary meanings in whatever language they find the most comfortable. Speakers of other languages might want to write definitions in their L_1.

The important work of these introductory sections is to help students understand the passage. Success with each lesson depends on understanding the ideas in the reading. Students who grasp ideas better in a language other than English should have opportunities, if possible, to discuss ideas in their L_1.

Listen and Practice

This is a mechanical drill and practice activity that prepares students to speak to the topic. Instructors will find it easier to complete this section if the audiocassette player to be used has a meter. Of course, you may read the passage as students complete each of the four activities. The best practice, however, is for students to hear several native speakers as they prepare for their work in the lesson. Steps c and d under "Listen" assist reluctant students in speaking out with minimum risk. You might decide to repeat one or both of these steps if students need more preparation.

ACTIVITIES FOR ODD-NUMBERED LESSONS

Memorize and Recite

Some learners enjoy memorizing. This section summarizes the reading passage in simple sentences. It will challenge some students who will be able to memorize only one or two phrases. They must be encouraged, however, to memorize the complete assignment.

Other students will find it easy to do the memorization. Reciting the lines will be difficult for some students, even those who memorize easily. These students may write the phrases to show that they have memorized them. They may say them chorally at their tables or with the entire class.

The memorization work can be done at home or in class. Learners for whom it is too easy can challenge themselves by memorizing an entire paragraph from the passage. There will even be students who decide to memorize the passage.

This is the end of the first section of the odd-numbered lessons. If you have dedicated enough time, as much as a half an hour, to the various oral activities, you will have given learners the greatest opportunity to have success in the rest of the lesson.

Paraphrase and Substitute

This activity guides students as they locate a phrase in the passage, circle it, copy the phrase, and copy it again, substituting the phrase in b. Follow these steps when presenting this exercise:

1. Model the example by saying it.

2. Model the example in writing.

3. Have students practice the exercises orally.

4. Have students write the exercises.

Students who complete this activity quickly may read the phrases they locate to one another.

Pair Work

Follow these steps to complete the **Pair Work** activity:

1. Model the first A and B questions with a student.

2. Students in pairs ask questions orally.

3. Students in pairs help one another complete the exercise in writing.

   The students who finish this exercise early should help the slower students. Some students will need to look at Student A's page and Student B's page simultaneously as they work towards being able to ask and answer questions using only oral cues.

The Guessing Game

This section aids learners in formulating questions. Follow these steps to complete the activity:

1. Put the first cues on the board.

   W _ _ _ s _ _ _ u_ t _ _ g _ _ _ _ _ _ _ _ _?

2. The class reads the response aloud.

3. Students call out words to complete the question.

4. Fill in the missing letters to complete the question, then erase the board.

5. Students work on each exercise orally.

6. Students write in the questions.

7. Student pairs take turns asking and answering the questions.

8. With students' books closed, read an answer.

9. Working in groups of four, students formulate the question.

10. One student verifies the question by looking in the book.

Give a Speech

This introduction to speaking in front of a group lets students talk to the largest group with which they feel comfortable. For some learners, this will mean a private audience with the instructor, or with a tape recorder.

   The activity emphasizes individual formal presentation ability. Only the most gregarious and self-confident learners will want to address an entire class in Lesson 1. Each student's goal should be to speak in front of a larger group at the end of Lesson 15 than they addressed at the end of Lesson 1.

ACTIVITIES FOR EVEN-NUMBERED LESSONS

Recite and Memorize

Teacher modeling is always very important. For this activity, model a complete exercise before students begin. The five facts can be copied, word for word, from the passage above them. More advanced students will be able to paraphrase lines from the passage. Make the ability to paraphrase a class goal, to be reached by Lesson 15. Pairs of students, one or both of whom find this material difficult, can copy the same facts and practice saying them.

Ask a Partner

In this activity learners will use the passage to elaborate on the topic of the lesson. Some learners will be able to do the lesson orally, without reference to the passage. For others, this will be a print-based activity. Newcomers, students with no prior formal schooling in English, would highlight text and copy from a classmate in order to participate in the lesson. Have students follow these steps to complete the activity:

1. Select a partner.

2. Read the first question.

3. The partner answers.

4. Have the student support the answer given by his or her partner.

5. The student points to the text of the passage from which the answer comes.

6. Have students work in pairs to complete the activity.

Make a List

In this summarizing activity pairs of students list five facts from the passage. This quick review prepares them for the more formal speaking activity at the end of the lesson. Partners can quickly highlight, copy, and read the facts to one another.

Think About It

Provide a model, as you do with every activity, especially during the first lessons in the book. Write topics on the board, and surround each topic with lists of facts.

An example from Lesson 2:

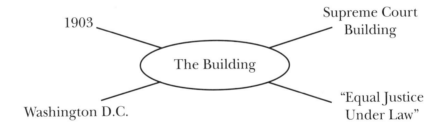

Explain as much about selecting a topic as the class will understand. Assign topics to students who are not familiar with the selection process.

For the conclusion activity, students can take ideas word for word from the passage. They can add visuals. Some may be able to locate additional information on the Internet and in books.

Give a Speech

For this activity three students team up to talk about and write down information about the topic. Each group should have enough time to prepare for the presentation. The preparation should include rehearsals alone as well as with the teacher. The final presentation can be to the teacher in the early lessons. Later, as students acquire more confidence, they can present to other groups or the whole class.

Extension Activities

Students who are reluctant to talk can do several activities while classmates prepare their presentations:

- Prepare illustrations for someone else's presentation. Because we are getting students ready to use language for effective communication, these illustrations will have to be thoroughly captioned and labeled; print should dominate.

- Transfer handwritten notes to the computer.

- Write scripts for other students to read.

- Record or videotape classmates' presentations.

- Prepare "strip stories" for classmates. To prepare a strip story, a student writes five to ten facts in sequential order, in large type. For example:

Many Americans had money in the 1920s.
The Depression was in the 1930s.
World War II was in the 1940s.
Many Americans got TVs in the 1950s.
Many students said no to war in the 1960s.

The student cuts the sentences and gives each sentence strip to a classmate. Each classmate who has a strip memorizes it. They then stand in front of the class, out of order, and say the sentence they have memorized. The students who are seated call out instructions to tell the students at the front of the room in what order they should stand.

As this is happening, the "audience" may require the speakers to repeat their sentences as often as necessary to achieve the correct arrangement. When the audience is satisfied, the five students repeat their statements, now presumably in the correct sequence.

- The seating chart: When determining a seating chart, turn the process into a challenging communicative assignment. Make a list of clues. Examples:

    John is to Marsha's right.

    Tu and Henry are on the same team.

    If Becky looks north, she will see Jayde.

Duplicate the clues, and give out 1/3 as many copies of the clues as there are students. Do not give clues to the reluctant speakers, nor to the most proficient third of the class. Students must read clues from the clues list; they may not show the list to another student. This activity works best with students who are not very disruptive. Be flexible when you schedule this activity! The students might surprise you, because this is an activity that could take from five to thirty minutes.

ANSWER KEY, BUILDING COMMUNICATION SKILLS FOR SOCIAL STUDIES

Answers are given where they are definitive. In many instances answers will vary. The integrated feature of the series means students will derive unique answers depending on how they respond to the questions.

LESSON 1: BRANCHES OF GOVERNMENT

Focus Questions (Page 1)
1. They're listening.
2. in the city

Paraphrase and Substitute (Page 3)
1a. The Congress has two parts.
1b. The Congress is divided into two houses.
2a. The president names judges.
2b. The president appoints justices.
3a. They decide if a law follows it.
3b. They decide if a law adheres to it.

Pair Work: Student A (Page 3)
1. Constitutional law
2. the Senate
3. the Vice President

Pair Work: Student B (Page 4)
1. the House of Representatives
2. the Army, the Navy, the Air Force
3. more than 1,000

The Guessing Game (Page 4)
1. What sets up the government?
2. What branch makes the laws?
3. Which states send more representatives?
4. What do the judges study?

LESSON 2: THE SUPREME COURT

Focus Questions (Page 5)
1. Nine people
2. They're resting.

Ask a Partner (Page 7)
Answers may vary. Possible answers include the following.
1. The Supreme Court met in New York City.
2. In 1903 it got a new home in Washington, D.C.
3. "Equal Justice Under Law" are the words carved into the building.

4. Today there are nine judges. We call them justices.
5. Marshall was the first African-American justice on the Supreme Court.

LESSON 3: TOWARD THE TWENTIETH CENTURY

Focus Questions (Page 9)
1. a train and some covered wagons with horses
2. bad

Paraphrase and Substitute (Page 11)
1a. The United States had gone up to the Mississippi River.
1b. The United States extended as far as the Mississippi River.
2a. Factories made more goods.
2b. Factories increased production.

Pair Work: Student A (Page 11)
1. In the North
2. Christopher Latham Sholes
3. No, Native Americans were.

Pair Work: Student B (Page 12)
1. In the 1800s
2. More than 100
3. On reservations

The Guessing Game (Page 12)
1. What were factories called?
2. After 1880, where did most native peoples live?
3. What did trains move?
4. What was invented in 1889?

LESSON 4: NEW STATES AND TERRITORIES

Focus Questions (Page 13)
1. You see mountains in Alaska.
2. There are palm trees in Hawaii.

Ask a Partner (Page 15)
Answers may vary. Possible answers include the following.
1. In 1867, the United States bought Alaska from Russia.
2. In 1898 the United States took over Hawaii.
3. In 1959, Hawaii became a state.

LESSON 5: MODERN CONVENIENCES

Pair Work: Student A (Page 19)
1. He was a speech teacher.
2. By phone
3. More than 1,000
4. CDs

Pair Work: Student B (Page 20)
1. North Carolina
2. About 250 meters.
3. The car
4. Flyer III

The Guessing Game (Page 20)
1. Who flew a plane?
2. What did Alexander Graham Bell invent?
3. What did Thomas Alva Edison invent?

LESSON 6: EARLY WORKING CONDITIONS

Focus Questions (Page 21)
1. No, she doesn't.
2. yes

Ask a Partner (Page 23)
Answers may vary. Possible answers include the following.
1. Some children spent 16 hours a day at work.
2. People on strike did not earn money.
3. Some children do not go to school.
4. In other countries, children work hard and make goods. Americans buy them.

LESSON 7: THE DUST BOWL

Focus Questions (Page 25)
1. four people
2. no

Paraphrase and Substitute (Page 27)
1a. This area goes from Canada to Texas.
1b. This area extends from Canada to Texas.
2a. In the 1920s the farms did well.
2b. In the 1920s agriculture did well.
3a. In the 1920s the farms did well.
3b. In the 1920s the farms prospered.
4a. In the 1930s there was a drought.
4b. In the 1930s there was a dry spell.
5a. From 1935 to 1940, families moved.
5b. From 1935 to 1940, families relocated.
6a. They left Colorado, Kansas, Oklahoma, Texas, and New Mexico.
6b. They abandoned Colorado, Kansas, Oklahoma, Texas, and New Mexico.

Pair Work: Student A (Page 27)
1. In the Great Plains
2. It was dry.
3. During the 1930s
4. Colorado, Oklahoma, Texas, Kansas, and New Mexico

Pair Work: Student B (Page 28)
1. It was free.
2. From wells
3. Five years
4. No rain

The Guessing Game (Page 28)
1. What grows on the Great Plains?
2. What is made from wheat?
3. When was the Homestead Act passed?

LESSON 8: WAR ON ICE

Focus Questions (Page 29)
1. They're angry.
2. They're fighting.

Ask a Partner (Page 31)
Answers may vary. Possible answers include the following.
1. The Cold War was after World War II.
2. The Cold War lasted almost 50 years.
3. The United States wanted a free world.
4. The Soviet Union wanted a communist world.
5. Both countries made bombs.

LESSON 9: CIVIL RIGHTS

Focus Questions (Page 33)
1. taking fingerprints
2. a police officer

Paraphrase and Substitute (Page 35)
1a. The Civil Rights Act of 1866 said black people were free.
1b. The Civil Rights Act of 1866 declared freedom for black people.
2a. When Woodrow Wilson was President, blacks lost jobs.
2b. When Woodrow Wilson served as President, blacks lost jobs.
3a. They worked apart from whites.
3b. They were segregated at work from whites.
4a. It was about separate schools.
4b. It concerned separate schools.
5a. She sat down.
5b. She took a seat.

Pair Work: Student A (Page 35)
1. 1866
2. When Wilson was President
3. Government jobs
4. The Supreme Court
5. Separation
6. No more segregation

Pair Work: Student B (Page 36)
1. Rosa Parks
2. In Alabama
3. Dr. Martin Luther King, Jr.
4. A boycott
5. The city buses
6. People who believed in civil rights

The Guessing Game (Page 36)
1. What did the Civil Rights Act of 1866 say?
2. Who could not vote?
3. Who led black people?
4. What did he say no to?

LESSON 10: OUT IN SPACE

Focus Questions (Page 37)
1. leaving the launch pad
2. going out in space

Ask a Partner (Page 39)
Answers may vary. Possible answers include the following:
1. The United States was not the first country in space.
2. The Soviet Union launched Sputnik I in 1957.
3. In 1961, the United States sent Alan B. Shepard into space.
4. In 1962 the United States put John Glenn into orbit.
5. In 1969 Neil Armstrong walked on the moon.

LESSON 11: WETLANDS

Paraphrase and Substitute (Page 43)
1a. People visit wetlands.
1b. People go there on vacation.
2a. But now twenty-two states have lost more than one-half of their wetlands.
2b. But now twenty-two states have lost more than 50 percent of their wetlands.
3a. Highways cross wetlands.
3b. Highways go through wetlands.
4a. Everyone wants to take trips.
4b. Everyone wants to travel.
5a. That's why towns and cities need more roads.
5b. That's why communities need more roads.

Pair Work: Student A (Page 43)
1. Homes.
2. In the 1700s
3. Highways
4. Plants and animals
5. The United States loses wetlands.

Pair Work: Student B (Page 44)
1. To work, to school, and to shop
2. In the 1990s
3. By computer
4. Ridesharing
5. By bike

The Guessing Game (Page 44)
1. What do wetlands house?
2. When were there more wetlands?
3. When did people start telecommuting?

LESSON 12: BURNED OUT

Ask a Partner (Page 47)
Answers may vary. Possible answers include the following:
1. Fire is bad. It kills trees.
2. It kills birds.
3. It kills people.
4. Sometimes people start fires.
5. Sometimes nature starts them.

LESSON 13: MOTHER EARTH

Paraphrase and Substitute (Page 51)
1a. In 1970 the first Earth Day was celebrated.
1b. In 1970 the first Earth Day was held.
2a. In 1896 they talked about the greenhouse effect.
2b. In 1896 they became aware of the greenhouse effect.
3a. That means the earth is getting warmer.
3b. That means the earth's temperature is rising.
4a. In 1992 many countries met.
4b. In 1992 many countries held a meeting.
5a. The United States uses more energy than other countries.
5b. The United States consumes more energy than other countries.

Pair Work: Student A (Page 51)
1. It's getting dirty.
2. Environmentalists
3. The environment
4. 1970
5. 1872
6. 1896

1. In 1992.
2. Brown
3. On farms
4. In and near cities
5. Factories
6. Take shorter showers

The Guessing Game (Page 52)
1. What is getting dirty?
2. What is around us?
3. When was the first Earth Day?
4. When did many countries meet in Brazil?

LESSON 14: HEALTH CARE

Ask a Partner (Page 55)
Answers may vary. Possible answers include the following:
1. Garfield liked to help people.
2. Some could not pay.
3. Garfield and another man made a plan.
4. The people would pay before they got sick.
5. They started Kaiser Permanente.

LESSON 15: THE NEIGHBORS

Paraphrase and Substitute (Page 59)
1a. People move there from all over the world.
1b. People immigrate from all over the world.
2a. The first Canadians were the Indian peoples.
2b. The original Canadians were the Indian peoples.
3a. Now they could not hunt.
3b. Now they were not able to hunt.
4a. Most came from Spain.
4b. The largest number came from Spain
5a. Spain controlled Mexico from the early 1500s to the early 1800s.
5b. Spain took over Mexico from the early 1500s to the early 1800s.

Pair Work: Student A (Page 59)
1. 1867
2. 1881
3. 1892
4. English and French
5. Indian peoples
6. By hunting

Pair Work: Student B (Page 60)
1. From the early 1500s to the early 1800s
2. In 1821
3. In 1917
4. In the 1840s
5. Faster
6. To find jobs

The Guessing Game (Page 60)
1. When did Canada build a railroad?
2. When did Canada get a new constitution?
3. When did Mexico write a new constitution?

BUILDING MAP SKILLS FOR SOCIAL STUDIES

INTRODUCTION

Americans' geographic illiteracy is well publicized. In *Building Map Skills for Social Studies*, you will find exercises and activities to assist students as they acquire an awareness of where they are in relation to the rest of the physical and cultural world. Students will be able to place events where they happened. They will read and interpret maps. Through these activities, students will develop a basis for making decisions and for asking and answering the big questions about our world.

In 1984 several organizations developed *Guidelines for Geographic Education*. This joint venture is called The Geographic Education National Implementation Project (GENIP). Members include the American Geographical Society, the Association of American Geographers, the National Council for Geographic Education, and the National Geographic Society. They organized geography study into five fundamental themes: location, place, human-environment interactions, movement, and regions. GENIP describes **location** as the where of geography, a place and its position relative to other locations and features. **Place** distinguishes a location by its physical and human features. **Human-environment interactions** describe the changes people make in our environment, and the consequences of these changes. **Movement** is the theme that addresses the relocation of goods and people, and the effects of this relocation. **Regions** is the theme that directs the study of physical and human characteristics that distinguish one section of a country or a continent from another.

Each of the lessons in this book develops around one of the five themes identified by GENIP. Maps are to geography what basic math operations are to mathematics. Students will use maps as a tool to acquire basic skills that will enable them to explore the five fundamental geography themes.

The National Council for Geographic Education continues to update guidelines for geography education with publications such as *Geography for Life*. This source helps teachers figure out how to help students think like geographers, see the "big picture," and perceive relationships between the physical world and its human inhabitants. As state initiatives play a larger role in shaping what and how we teach, the organizations mentioned above provide ongoing assistance in establishing and maintaining ever higher standards in geography teaching.

HOW TO USE THIS BOOK

Because Building Map Skills for Social Studies contains many short lessons, the Contents page appears here to give you an overview of the book. Lessons are grouped to develop map skills and to apply those skills to topics in United States Social Studies. Basic skill lessons appear at the beginning. History topics are arranged chronologically. You can select lessons by topic or by lesson theme to coordinate with the mainstream curriculum.

CONTENTS

EXTENSION ACTIVITIES

Lesson 1 Location: Continents and Borders

• Select other countries, and remove the borders with correction fluid; or use a computer. Students replace the borders.

• Students add the homelands of their ancestors to the continent maps on page 2.

Lesson 2 Location: Abbreviations

• Students find abbreviations for other places, for example, "Fr." for France.

• After completing the lesson, students cover the abbreviations with a piece of paper on which they write the abbreviations they have remembered.

Lesson 3 Movement: Migration

- Using outline maps of the United States, students trace important migrations such as the Oregon Trail.

- Bring map puzzles and map games such as Fly Away to class. Students play the games and assemble the puzzles.

Lesson 4 Location: North, South, East, and West

- Students label all eight directions in the classroom.

- Students describe where they are sitting in relation to other students: David sits to the east of Jennie.

Lesson 5 Place: Your Place

- Students write and illustrate descriptions of economic activity in your area. Consider agriculture, industry, and tourism.

- Students map connections your place has with surrounding areas: In the summer we go to _____ Lake west of here to swim. People who live here go to a discount warehouse in _____ to shop.

Lesson 6 Location: "Square" States

- Students draw an outline of any one of the states. They add several cities and describe their relative locations.

- Students illustrate and describe architecture, waterways, mountains, and weather in the given location.

Lesson 7 Regions: Mountains

- Students find the closest mountain range. They make a map that shows your location with respect to the mountain range. This can be a relief map.

- Students investigate the activity on this range. Is there skiing? mining? Are there resorts? parks? hiking trails? Using a map key, students create a map that shows where the activity takes place.

Lesson 8 Place: Immigrants in the United States

- Students search the Internet for immigration information. One source is the Immigration and Naturalization Service. They can graph tabulated data from the Service.

- Students make a map like the one on page 18, on which they place local immigration information.

Lesson 9 Human-Environment Interactions: The 1930s

- Students design a map key and map local landscape or agriculture uses.

- In pairs or groups, students prepare an expository essay on how local waterways are used. After they revise their essays, assemble the final copies in a class book.

Lesson 10 Movement: The New York Port Authority

- In teams, students research and create a stand-alone display of local transportation options. They present their projects to the class.

- Students select a single local means of transportation. They investigate schedules and make or copy route maps.

Lesson 11 Movement: The Interstate Highway System, North and South   AND
Lesson 12 Movement: The Interstate Highway System, East and West

- On the Internet, students find maps of the cities in these lessons. They look at the highways that cross these cities.

- Students construct a three-dimensional map of your area, showing major roadways.

Lesson 13 Place: Chicago O'Hare International Airport

- Take the class to an airport. Check out air routes, shuttle routes, and other maps of airport-related activity.

- Students make travel inquiries on the Internet. Then they report to the class on schedules and fares.

Lesson 14 Regions: Four National Parks

- Show students the National Parks' homepages on the Internet. In pairs, students select a national park and present information about it.

- Lead a discussion of what makes a good national park. What physical features should be present? How do humans play a role?

Lesson 15 Location: The Presidents' Home States

- Students use the list on pages 35 and 36 and an outline map of the entire United States to show the presidents' home states.

- Students research the vice presidents and their home states. They compile a list like the one on pages 35 and 36.

Lesson 16 Movement: Great Lakes Ports

- Students bring boxes or cans of food to class. They read the labels to learn where the product was packaged or produced. Then they map this information.

- Invite local store managers to class. Have maps available for them to show students where they get the products they sell.

Lesson 17 Human-Environment Interactions: Panama Canal Zone

- Students research a local road or waterway that changed the landscape and shortened a route between two locations.

- Guide students as they list the advantages and disadvantages of shortening a route such as New York to California.

Lesson 18 Human-Environment Interactions: Ski Resorts

- Students list and map a popular resort in your area.

- Students prepare a descriptive paragraph telling how a site was altered to accommodate a sport.

Lesson 19 Place: Watersheds

- Students research the nearest river. Is it clean enough for fishing, swimming or even as a source of drinking water?

- Take students to the closest body of water and help them test the water with a simple water-testing kit.

Lesson 20 Human-Environment Interactions: Acid Rain

- Take students to a local factory to research how the factory controls pollutants. They should bring clipboards and prepared questions for the factory representative.

- For a display, have students illustrate the path of pollutants from a factory, through the air, and back to earth as rain.

Lesson 21 Location: Latitude and Longitude

- Students map their location on a grid, showing latitude and longitude lines.

- Give students coordinates for major cities, and have them locate the cities.

Lesson 22 Place: Estuaries

- Students select an estuary and determine what plants and animals live there.

- Students illustrate a river, labeling the source, the estuary, and the ocean into which it empties.

Lesson 23 Movement: Japanese Autos in the United States

- In the school parking lot, students list twenty vehicles and the countries that produce them.

- On the Internet, students visit the different automobile manufacturers' homepages.

Lesson 24 Location: Change the Scale

- Pairs of students use transparent grids and graph paper to change the scale of drawings of different states.

- Using a computer, students download the outline of a state. Then they enlarge it and reduce it. More advanced students will enlarge two neighboring states, then place them together on the page.

ANSWER KEY, BUILDING MAP SKILLS FOR SOCIAL STUDIES

Answers are given where they are definitive. In many instances answers
will vary. The integrated feature of the series means students will derive unique answers depending on how they respond to the questions.

LESSON 1 LOCATION: CONTINENTS AND BORDERS

B. (Page 2)

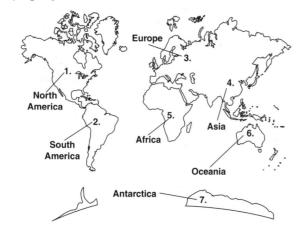

LESSON 2 LOCATION: ABBREVIATIONS

(Page 3)
Answers to the first two questions will vary with each class.

The names of the states and territories are

Alaska	Alabama
Arkansas	Arizona
California	Colorado
Connecticut	Delaware
Florida	Georgia
Hawaii	Iowa
Idaho	Illinois
Indiana	Kansas
Kentucky	Louisiana
Massachusetts	Maryland
Maine	Michigan
Minnesota	Missouri
Mississippi	Montana
North Carolina	North Dakota
Nebraska	New Hampshire
New Jersey	New Mexico
Nevada	Now York
Ohio	Oklahoma
Oregon	Pennsylvania
Rhode Island	South Carolina
South Dakota	Tennessee
Texas	Utah
Virginia	Vermont
Washington	Wisconsin
West Virginia	Wyoming
Puerto Rico	Virgin Islands
Marshall Islands	American Samoa
District of Columbia	Guam

LESSON 3 MOVEMENT: MIGRATION
Answers will vary for both questions on page 5.

A, B, and C. (Page 6)
Students' maps will vary for all three activities.

LESSON 4 LOCATION: NORTH, SOUTH, EAST, AND WEST
Students' answers to what is north, south, east, and west of them will vary.

A. (Page 7)
Top line: GHI; second line: MNO; third line: XYZ; fourth line: ABC

B. (Page 7)
Top line: JKL; second line: QRS; third line: MNO; fourth line: ABC

C. (Page 8)
The order should be (from left to right) DEF, ABC, JKL, and GHI.

D. (Page 8)
The order should be (from left to right) XYZ, RST, UVW, and ABC.

E. (Page 8)

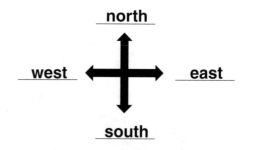

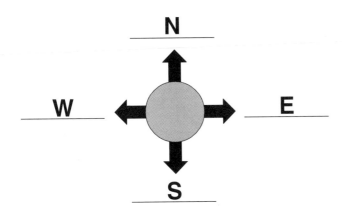

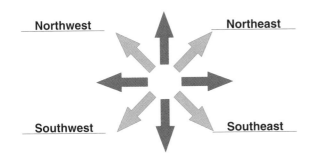

F. (Page 9)

G. (Page 9)

LESSON 5 PLACE: YOUR PLACE

A. (Page 10)
Answers to the fill-in-the-blank question and to items 1 through 5 will vary.

B. (Page 10)
Answers for items 1 through 5 will vary for each student.

C. (Pages 10–11)
Students' maps will vary.

LESSON 6 LOCATION: "SQUARE" STATES

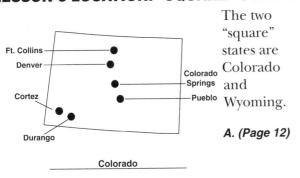

The two "square" states are Colorado and Wyoming.

A. (Page 12)

B. (Page 13)

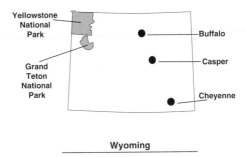

LESSON 7 REGIONS: MOUNTAINS

(Pages 14–15)
Answers to the first two questions will vary for each class.

Mountain Ranges

LESSON 8 PLACE: IMMIGRANTS IN THE UNITED STATES

Answers to the first three questions on page 16 will vary.

A. (Page 16)

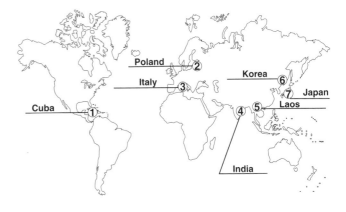

B. (Page 17)

Country	Symbol
Cuba	C
India	In
Italy	It
Japan	J
Korea	K
Laos	L
Poland	P

C. (Pages 17–18)

Where Some Immigrants Settled in the 1900s

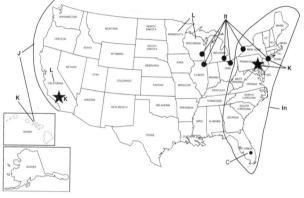

LESSON 9 HUMAN-ENVIRONMENT INTERACTIONS: THE 1930S

Answers to questions 1 and 2 on page 19 will vary.
3. Plants need water, good soil, sunlight, and nutrients (like fertilizer) to grow.

A, B, C, and D. (Pages 19–20)

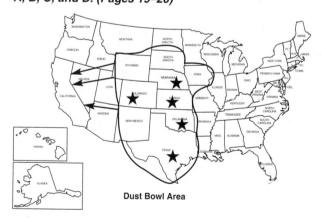

Dust Bowl Area

A. (Page 21)

Parts of the following states are included within the shaded line: Virginia, North Carolina, Tennessee, Georgia, Alabama, Mississippi, and Kentucky.

B, C, D. (Page 21)

LESSON 10 MOVEMENT: THE NEW YORK PORT AUTHORITY

A and B. (Page 22)

C. (Page 23)

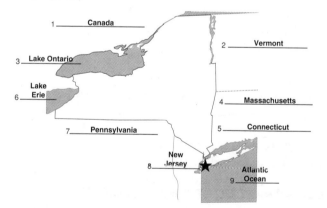

1. Canada
2. Vermont
3. Lake Ontario
4. Massachusetts
5. Connecticut
6. Lake Erie
7. Pennsylvania
8. New Jersey
9. Atlantic Ocean

D. (Page 24)

LESSON 11 MOVEMENT: THE INTERSTATE HIGHWAY SYSTEM, NORTH AND SOUTH

A, B, C, D, E, and F. (Pages 25–26)

A.

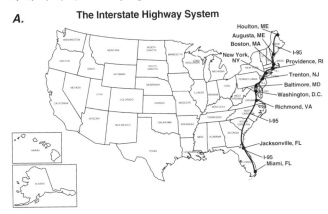

B.

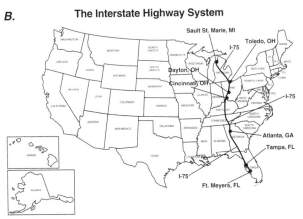

C.

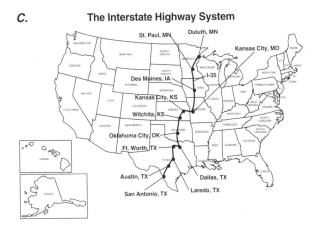

D.

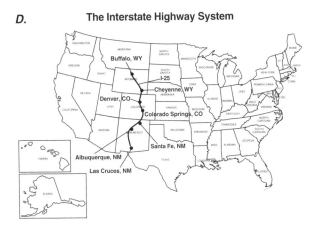

E.

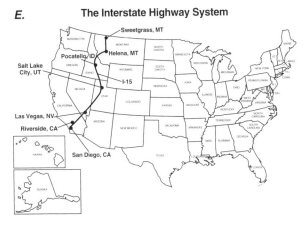

F.

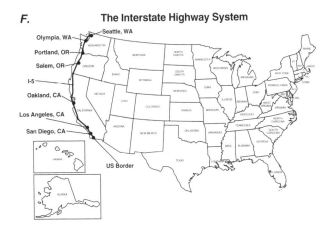

G. (Page 26)

These highways run north and south in the United States. They are numbered in increments of 10 beginning with 5. The lower numbers are in the West.

LESSON 12 MOVEMENT: THE INTERSTATE HIGHWAY SYSTEM, EAST AND WEST

A, B, C, D, E, and F. (Pages 27–28)

A.

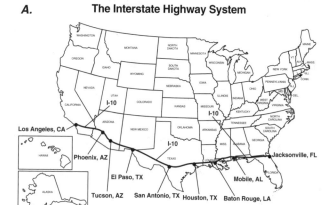

The Interstate Highway System

B.

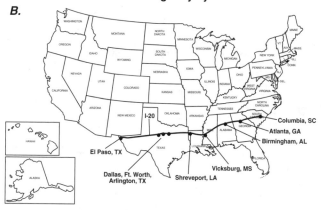

The Interstate Highway System

C.

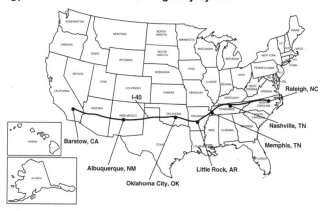

The Interstate Highway System

D.

The Interstate Highway System

E.

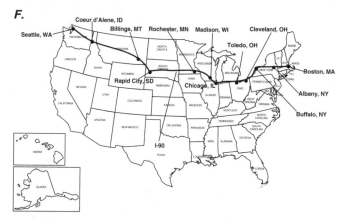

The Interstate Highway System

F.

H. (Page 28)

These highways run horizontally across the map of the United States. They are numbered in increments of 10 starting with 10. The numbers are low in the south, high in the north.

LESSON 13 PLACE: CHICAGO O'HARE INTERNATIONAL AIRPORT

B. (Page 30)

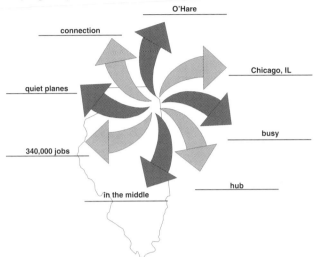

LESSON 14 REGIONS: FOUR NATIONAL PARKS

A. (Pages 31–32)

Hawaii

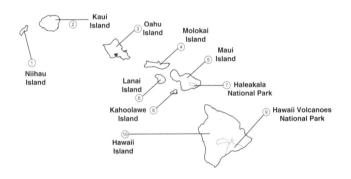

B. (Page 33)
1. Haleakala National Park
   Maui, Hawaii
   1961
   It was part of Hawaii Volcanoes National Park.
2. Hawaii Volcanoes National Park
   Hawaii, Hawaii
   1916
   It has two active volcanoes.
3. National Park of American Samoa
   Pago Pago, American Samoa
   1988
   It has special animals and birds and
   a rain forest.
4. War in the Pacific National Historic Park
   Guam
   1978
   It is on the ocean.

C. (Pages 33–34)

Map of World

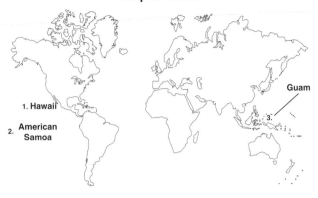

D. (Page 34)

Map of Oceania

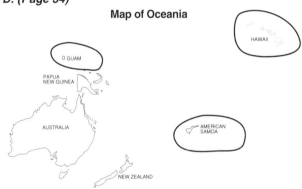

LESSON 15 LOCATION: THE PRESIDENTS' HOME STATES

(Pages 35–36)
1. No
2. New York
Arkansas
William J. Clinton
1993–
California

Herbert C. Hoover
1929–1933
Richard M. Nixon
1969–1974
Georgia
James E. Carter
1977–1981

(Page 36)
Illinois
Abraham Lincoln
1861–1865
Ulysses S. Grant
1869–1877
Ronald Reagan
1981–1989
Louisiana
Zachary Taylor
1849–1850
Massachusetts
John Adams
1797–1801
John Quincy Adams
1825–1829

Calvin Coolidge
1923–1929
John F. Kennedy
1961–1963
Michigan
Gerald R. Ford
1974–1977
Missouri
Harry S Truman
1945–1953
New Hampshire
Franklin Pierce
1853–1857

(Page 37)
New Jersey
Woodrow Wilson
1913–1921
New York
Martin Van Buren
1830–1841
Millard Fillmore
1850–1853
Chester A. Arthur
1881–1885
Grover Cleveland
1885–1889 and
    1893–1897
Benjamin Harrison
1889–1893
Theodore Roosevelt
1901–1909

Franklin D. Roosevelt
1933–1945
Dwight D. Eisenhower
1953–1961
Ohio
William Henry
    Harrison
1841–1841
Rutherford B. Hayes
1877–1881
James A. Garfield
1881–1881
William McKinley
1897–1901
William Howard Taft
1909–1913
Warren G. Harding
1921–1923

(Page 38)
Pennsylvania
James Buchanan
1857–1861
Tennessee
Andrew Jackson
1829–1837
James K. Polk
1845–1849
Andrew Johnson
1865–1869
Virginia
George Washington
1789–1797

Thomas Jefferson
1801–1809
James Madison
1809–1817
James Monroe
1817–1825
John Tyler
1841–1845
Texas
Lyndon B. Johnson
1963–1969
George Bush
1989–1993

LESSON 16 MOVEMENT: GREAT LAKES PORTS

Sample answer for question 1 on page 39: boat, plane, train, truck
Answers to the second question will vary.

A. (Page 39)

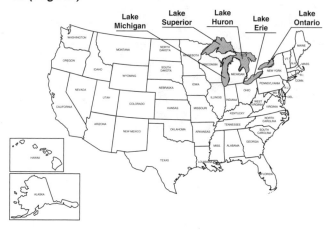

B. (Page 40)

The states are: (top row, left to right) Illinois, Indiana, and Ohio; (bottom row, left to right) Minnesota and Wisconsin.

C. (Page 40)

Chicago, Illinois   Burns Harbor, Indiana
Huron, Ohio / Toledo, Ohio
Duluth, Minnesota   Superior, WI / Milwaukee, WI

D. (Page 41)

Great Lakes Ports

LESSON 17 HUMAN-ENVIRONMENT INTERACTIONS: PANAMA CANAL ZONE

Answers to the first two questions on page 42 will vary.

A. (Pages 42–43)

B and C. (Page 44)

LESSON 18 HUMAN-ENVIRONMENT INTERACTIONS: SKI RESORTS

(Page 45)
Some states that have ski resorts are:

Maine	West Virginia	NewMexico
Vermont	North Carolina	Idaho
New Hampshire	Ohio	Utah
Massachusetts	Michigan	Arizona
Connecticut	Wisconsin	Washington
New Jersey	Minnesota	Oregon
New York	Montana	Nevada
Pennsylvania	Wyoming	California
Virginia	Colorado	

LESSON 19 PLACE: WATERSHEDS

A and B. (Pages 47–48)

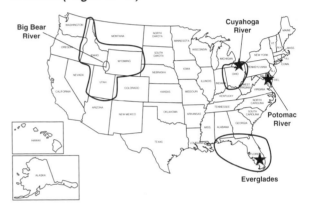

LESSON 20 HUMAN-ENVIRONMENT INTERACTIONS: ACID RAIN

A and B. (Pages 49–50)

LESSON 21 LOCATION: LATITUDE AND LONGITUDE

Answers to the first two questions on page 51 will vary for each class. Question 3: The South Pole is at 90° south latitude (90°S).

A. (Page 52)

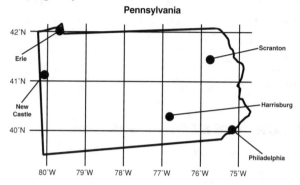
Pennsylvania

Erie is 42° N and east of 80°W.

B. (Page 53)
Louisiana.

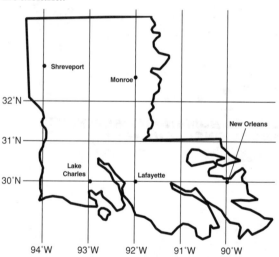

C, D, and E. (Page 54)

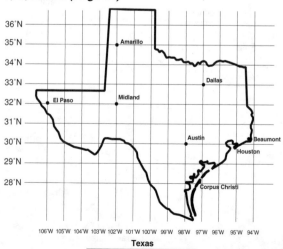
Texas

LESSON 22 PLACE: ESTUARIES

A and B. (Pages 55–56)

Estuaries

C. (Page 57)

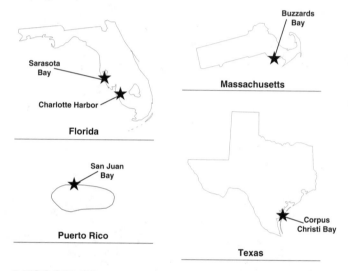

LESSON 23 MOVEMENT: JAPANESE AUTOS IN THE UNITED STATES

(Page 58)

LESSON 24 LOCATION: CHANGE THE SCALE

a big map

A and B. (Pages 59–60)

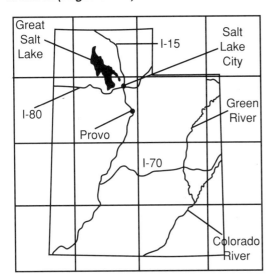

BUILDING MATH SKILLS FOR SOCIAL STUDIES

INTRODUCTION

Building Math Skills for Social Studies uses events in twentieth-century social studies as a backdrop for math lessons. The math lessons acknowledge the direction that the National Council of Teachers of Math standards provided to educational reform in the 1989 document *Curriculum and Evaluation Standards for School Mathematics*. The social studies link serves the "making connections" standard.

Each series of math activities is placed in a context to make it more accessible for learners. For students who seek meaning in math, who want to know why they must learn the operations and processes, *Building Math Skills for Social Studies* provides an answer. With across-the-curriculum lessons, this book sets math in an environment that provides learners with reasons for using math.

HOW TO USE THIS BOOK

Each lesson has these sections:

Calculation

The calculation section gives attention to basic math because some students have had little prior schooling. They need the same extensive practice that their classmates might have had. Calculator math helps basic math students survive while they catch up to their classmates in computational skills and prepare to work on more cognitively demanding problems.

Mental math, pencil and paper math, and calculator math provide warm-ups for the main part of the lesson, which begins with simple word problems. You will be able to use these problems to give students clues on the operations they need to use to answer the problems. They can highlight words such as "together" and "more than" in the questions. These words provide clues to which operation is the right one to solve the problem.

Math Tool

In this section learners use math tools to perform some kind of inquiry. Every day, students are surrounded with math tools, the operation of which they must master. Some examples are scales, metronomes, and rulers. In many of the lessons in the book, this section is linked to the following section.

Math Notation

While learners frequently are called on to read math notation, they lack practice in the process of making the notation themselves. A student who can set up a list, a tally sheet, or a graph gains experience in how these methods of recording data serve to synthesize information and make it easy to recover. When presented with math notation on tests and in texts, these students will be better equipped to study and interpret it.

Open-Ended Problems

An important feature of statewide assessments that accompany education reform is the open-ended math problem. Typically, the states expect students to discover two methods for solving the problem, to design a visual that explains the solution, and to provide a narrative that reveals how they thought about the problem while they were solving it.

Math students differ greatly in their training and abilities. These differences are so notable that schools governed by a philosophy of heterogeneous grouping often track or group students only for math! We find middle school students who still struggle with simple sums, and others who are comfortable with algebra and geometry. What follows is an activity-by-activity description of how to teach the first lesson. Each lesson in the book may be taught using the same procedures.

LESSON 1: IMMIGRATION

Beginning students can circle or highlight the numbers. Then, in pairs, students practice reading the numbers. A proficient reader may read the passage aloud for the class.

Some students will round the numbers easily, but all should write and read the answers. Choral reading helps reticent students learn to read the large numbers.

On page 2, transforming to and from numerals has application in check writing and general reading. Activity C can become a race if learners use calculators efficiently. Some students can beat a calculator, and this kind of competition serves to help students keep their math facts crisp. In Section 2, students might circle or highlight "altogether" in problem a, "come" and "leave" in problem b, and "in the three years" in problem c. That way they begin to recognize language that cues them to the different math operations.

Sections 3 and 4 consist of a chart in this lesson. Graphic organizers have applications in all the content areas. While learners are frequently directed to interpret charts and tables, they need to learn to design them. Both sections may be done individually, in pairs, or in small groups. In some classrooms the best way to complete these sections will be as a class.

The five parts of Section 5 provide practice in the skills that state assessments measure. These "open-ended" math problems typically range from easy to complex on the same test. They sometimes include extraneous information. To meet the state standard, students present two methods by which they solve the problem.

A visual component may accompany the computation. This could be an illustration, a chart, a tally sheet, or any other form of visual description that enhances the text of the student's answer.

A logical narrative is expected in which students delineate the thought processes that guide them as they work through the problem. Section D is a simple format for presenting the process. It gives learners practice in writing the narrative explanation. After completing their narratives, students should read them to one another. Once students appear confident and comfortable in the classroom, the teacher and classmates will be able to suggest improvements. The revision of Section 5, Part D, is an important exercise because it

- clarifies the math concepts,

- connects to the writing process,

- encourages a team effort among students, and

- prepares students to present a logical narrative on the statewide assessment.

Newcomer students will of course be unable to manage this work independently. They should copy the narrative from a proficient classmate. They may also do the computation, and redo it substituting different figures. This serves several purposes for the newcomer, who will practice computation, practice writing math problems, complete work similar to that of classmates, and practice sequential vocabulary for narrative explanations: "First . . . ," "Then . . . ," etc.

Finally, students who sit for the open-ended math assessment are expected to derive the correct answer, for which some credit is usually given. They should draw a box or circle around the answer to practice designating it for readers.

EXTENSION ACTIVITIES

Lesson 1: Immigration

- Students make inquiries into local immigration and/or migration patterns

- In communities where people of many nationalities live together, students rewrite the lesson with local statistics.

- In other communities students interview a realtor to rewrite the lesson using local migration patterns.

Lesson 2: The American Red Cross

- Students interview a representative of the local Red Cross, or any other service organization.

- They rewrite the lesson using local facts.

- Section 1, Part A, can become month-to-month practice: How many months (weeks, days) from February 1 to October 1? Transformations in Part B might look like this: 3/13/02–March 13, 2002.

Lesson 3: Suffrage

- Students repeat Sections 3 and 4 on page 12 with other topics. Some topics: sports, movies, classes.

- Invite an election worker to class to answer prepared questions. Record the session to review afterwards with students.

- Students find names of local government officials.

Lesson 4: The Roaring Twenties

- Listen to jazz.

- Make a table of local businesses and which credit cards they accept.

	Discover	Master Card	Visa	none
Ike's Bikes				
Allnite Bakery				
Ritemed Drugs				

- Demonstrate a metronome to check Section 4, page 17, calculations.

Lesson 5: The Great Depression

- Search the employment pages of a local newspaper. Highlight job titles and wages.

- Convert the information gathered above to a table.

Job Title	Wage
_____	_____
_____	_____
_____	_____

- Students develop a store theme such as a fast-food restaurant or a shoe store. They design a poster to display products and prices. With real or play money, students "shop" and make change. Shoppers and shopkeepers can check each transaction with paper and pencil or a calculator.

Lesson 6: Olympic Games

- In teams of three, learners select activities. Some examples: carrying a potato on a spoon across the room without holding or dropping it, or moving ten shelled peanuts, one by one, from a table to a plate, using chopsticks. Two team members perform the task, while the third member uses a stopwatch to time them. Each member of the team calculates the difference in time for each event. Then they compare answers.

- Using data on the Time Chart in Section 4, page 23, students select pairs of times and compute the differences.

- Students find more information on Jesse Owens. When was he born? Where? They look at a map or globe and find his birthplace.

Lesson 7: The New Deal

- In teams of six, students select an object to make. They assign five tasks to complete the object. One student times the "assembly line," while the other five make the object.

- They practice presenting, then present the project to another team or to the class.

- Students find Milwaukee, Wisconsin on a map. Using a map scale and a ruler, they estimate how far it is from their location.

Lesson 8: Duck® Tape

- Students locate three stores in your area that sell tape. They circle their location on a local map and make a table to show the kinds of tape each sells.

Store	Kinds of tape
Ace Supermarket	adhesive, masking, transparent
Mo's Pharmacy	medical, masking, Duck®

- Students interview a store manager. They ask, "How much tape do you sell each month?" Then they chart the quantity of tape sold and convert the answer to different units.

  Example:

      1 roll = 200 yards = 600 feet (etc.)

- Students locate France, Mt. Everest, and Washington, DC on a map and a globe.

Lesson 9: The United States Auto Industry

- In the school parking lot, students record car makes or sizes (compact, mid-size) on a paper attached to a clipboard. Each student can design a different tally sheet. Some might graph the data they record. Ask students to show their work to a small group or the class.

- Bring tape measures, yardsticks, meter sticks and rulers to class. Students formulate measurement problems for one another. These can follow the format of problems in Section 1, page 33, or Section 2, page 34.

- With a collection of toy cars and a scale, do an estimation activity. Students guess which cars are heavier than others, and line up the cars according to weight. Then they weigh each car to verify their guesses. Students can illustrate, chart, or graph the information.

Lesson 10: Warehouse Retail Stores

- Take a field trip to a local warehouse retail store. Students can ask a manager about the number of jobs at the store, how many items are sold there and how many other store branches the company has.

- Find out where ten or twelve branch stores are of the local warehouse retail store. Mark them on a map.

- Students copy Section 2 Word Problems, page 37, substituting different numbers. Then they give their new problems to someone else in the class to solve.

Lesson 11: Oil Spills

- Demonstrate an oil spill by pouring motor oil into a pan of water.

- Use measuring cups, water, and beans or rice to demonstrate the mental math activity in Section 1, Part A, page 40.

- Bring recipe books that contain measurement tables. Students can refer to these books to design or copy measurement tables for display in the classroom.

Lesson 12: Does the Sun Ever Set on the Disney Empire?

- Students visit a travel agent for a brochure on a theme park. They calculate the admission price if the entire class were to go.

- Students search for theme park statistics on the Internet.

- Students consult a biography of Walt Disney and prepare a presentation for the class. Encourage them to report on Disney using numbers. Examples: How long ago was he born? How far from his home did he build the first theme park?

Lesson 13: IBM Plays Chess

- Students play a chess game. They can also organize a chess club or tournament in the classroom or in the school.

- If a computer chess game is available, students who know how to play the game can demonstrate it for their classmates.

- Try Section 2, page 50, with four students from the class. Have them stand in front of the class and demonstrate the different line formations.

Lesson 14: Topic For the 90s: Global Warming

- Check a local newspaper for local temperatures, or temperatures in another city. Chart them for a week.

- Watch a weather report on TV. How much data can students take down during the weather report? If they put their individual notes together, can they reconstruct the report?

- Graph annual average temperature highs and lows. These data can often be found toward the back of any American Automobile Association Tour Book.

Lesson 15: "As the Crow Flies"—Our National Parks

- Students inquire about the closest regional or national park. When did it open? How large is it? They write a description of the park from the information they get, or they describe a park they have visited.

- On a map or globe, students locate each national park mentioned in the passage. Then they tell which park they would like to visit, and why.

- Students select pairs of cities on a map and determine the distance between each pair.

ANSWER KEY, BUILDING MATH SKILLS FOR SOCIAL STUDIES

Answers are given where they are definitive. In many instances answers will vary. The integrated feature of the series means students will derive unique answers depending on how they respond to the questions.

LESSON 1: IMMIGRATION

1A. Mental Math (Page 1)

8,796,000	2,516,000
5,737,000	3,322,000
4,108,000	4,494,000
528,000	7,338,000
1,036,000	5,231,000

1B. Pencil and Paper Math (Page 2)

1,025,671

528,037

2,515,944

3,322,374

eight million, seven hundred ninety-five thousand, eight hundred eighty-eight
five million, seven hundred thirty-six thousand, six hundred seventy-one
five million, two hundred thirty thousand, six hundred sixty-five

1C. Calculator Math (Page 2)

1995 total: 1,410,101

1996 total: 1,677,414

1997 total: 2,274,948

1998 total: 2,445,082

1999 total: 2,007,671

2. Word Problems (Page 3)
   a. 509,677 people
   b. 4,745 people
   c. 54,442 people

3. Math Tools (Page 3)

Year	Country 1	Country 2	Country 3	Total
1995	357,000	398,000	655,000	1,410,000
1996	303,000	468,000	907,000	1,677,000
1997	436,000	545,000	1,294,000	2,275,000
1998	532,000	336,000	1,577,000	2,445,000
1999	207,000	312,000	1,489,000	2,008,000

4. Math Notation (Page 4)

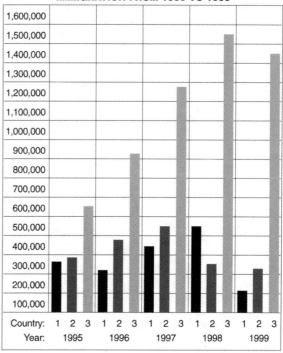

IMMIGRATION FROM 1995 TO 1999

5. Open-Ended Problem (Page 5)
A. Do the Math
Suggested answer:

	3,575	doctors
	7,280	engineers
+	7,500	refugees
	18,355	

	20,000	total
−	18,355	
	1,645	

B. Do It Another Way

20,000	total number of immigrants from Country Y
− 3,575	doctors
16,425	
− 7,280	engineers
9,145	
− 7,500	refugees
1, 645	

C. Let's Look At It

Doctors and Engineers	Refugees	Other
20,000	10,855	7,500	1,645

D. Explain the Math (Page 6)
Suggested Answer:
First, I read the problem and decided to add and then subtract.
Then I added the number of doctors to the number of engineers.
Next, I added the number of refugees to the total. After that, I subtracted this total from 20,000, the number of immigrants that Country X would take.
Finally, I checked my answer by starting with the total and subtracting.

E. Write the Answer

> 1,645 people

LESSON 2: THE AMERICAN RED CROSS

1A. Mental Math (Page 7)
1 year
19 years
23 years
17 years
16 years
4 years

1B. Pencil and Paper Math (Page 7)
1863

1864

1881

Nineteen hundred

Nineteen sixteen

Nineteen eighteen

Nineteen forty-one

Nineteen forty-five

2. Word Problems (Page 8)
a. 23 years
b. 6 to 7 years
c. 19 years

5. Open-Ended Problem (Page 9)
A. Do the Math

21	families have another house.
13	families can stay with relatives.
18	families can stay with friends.
+ 125	families found a place with the Red Cross
177	families have a place to stay.
200	
− 177	
23	families still need a place to live.

B. Do It Another Way

200	total families lost their homes
− 21	families have another house.
179	
− 13	families can stay with relatives.
166	
− 18	families can stay with friends.
148	
− 125	families found a place with the Red Cross
23	families still need a place to live.

C. Let's Look At It

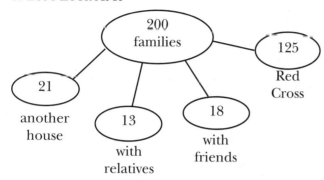

D. Explain the Math (Page 10)
First, I studied the problem and decided to add, then subtract.
Then I added the families who had another house, the number of families who could stay with friends, and the families who could stay with relatives.
Next, I added the number of families who got a place to stay from the Red Cross.
After that, I subtracted the number of people who had places to stay from 200, the number of people who lost their homes.
Finally, I checked my addition and subtraction.

E. Write the Answer

23 people

LESSON 3: SUFFRAGE

1A. Mental Math (Page 11)
17 years	4 years	8 years
8 years	4 years	8 years

1B. Pencil and Paper Math (Page 11)
55   59   68   55

1C. Calculator Math (Page 11)
66   73
53   56

2. Word Problems (Page 11)
a. 52 years old
b. 55 years old
c. 108 years

5. Open-Ended Problem (Page 13)
Students might change figures based on assumptions, i.e., women who do not want the ball field will vote for it for their sons. Extraneous information: number of women on team.

A. Do the Math

  2,500 total number of voters (women only)
−   700 want the field
_____

  1,800 voters (women only)
         do not want the field.

    700 women want the field
 1,075 men want the field
+   23 team members want the field
_____

 1,798 voters (men and women) want the field

B. Do It Another Way

  2,500 total number of voters (women only)
−   700 want the field
_____

  1,800 voters (women only)
         do not want the field.

1,800 > 700

  2,000 total number of voters (men only)
  1,098 men want the field
(1,075 not on team + 23 on team)
_____

   902 voters (men only) do not want the field

   902 voters (men only) do not want the field.
+ 1800 voters (women only) do not want the field.
_____

  2,702 voters (men and women) do not want the field, 1,798 do want the field.

2,702 > 1,798

C. Let's Look At It

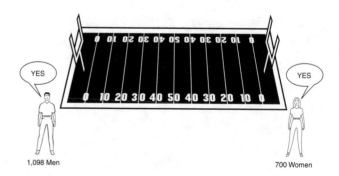

D. Explain the Math (Page 14)

First, I read the problem and decided to use subtraction and addition.

Then I subtracted the number of women who wanted the field from the total number of women voters.

Next, I added the number of men and women together and subtracted the number of women who wanted the field.

After that, I subtracted the number of men who wanted the field from the total above.

Finally, I checked my answer by doing it another way.

E. Write the Answer

No
No

LESSON 4: THE ROARING TWENTIES

1A. Mental Math (Page 15)

60	60	60
60	120	60

1B. Pencil and Paper Math (Page 15)

1. $60,000,000
2. $850,000,000
3. $15.00
4. $80,000
5. $400,000
6. $16,000,000

eleven dollars

seventy million dollars

eighteen million dollars

five hundred thousand dollars

six hundred forty million dollars

1C. Calculator Math (Page 16)

$260,000	$698,500
$25,619	$49,893
$22,079	$34,676

2. Word Problems (Page 16)

1. $790 million
2. February 1931

4. Math Notation (Page 17)

90/60	130/60
100/60	45/60
120/60	50/60

5. Open-Ended Problem (Page 17)

A. Do the Math

Possible answers include:

	$12,000	Used Car
	3,000	New Computer
	1,200	New Refrigerator
	600	New Washer
+	900	Used Radio

$17,700 Total Amount Spent

B. Do It Another Way (Page 18)

	$20,000	
−	12,000	Used Car

	$8,000	
−	3,000	New Computer

	$5,000	
−	1,200	New Refrigerator

	$3,800	
−	600	New Washer

	$3,200	
−	900	Used Radio

$2,300

C. Let's Look At It

	New	Used
	$19,000	$12,000
	$3,000	$900
	$1,200	$800
	$600	$400
	$3,000	$900

D. Explain the Math

Suggested Answer:

First, I studied the problem .

Then, I decided what to buy new and what to buy used.

Next, I started adding prices to get close to $20,000. I knew I wanted a new computer.

After that, I added the prices of a new refrigerator and a new washer to the total .

Finally, I checked my answer by subtracting.

E. Write the Answer

I will buy	New	Used
A car		$12,000
A computer	$3,000	
A refrigerator	$1,200	
A washer	$600	
A radio		$900

LESSON 5: THE GREAT DEPRESSION

1A. Mental Math (Page 19)

$5,000 $4,000

$5,000 $20,200

1B. Pencil and Paper Math (Page 19)

$4,833

$7,920

$9,973

$10,166

1C. Calculator Math (Page 19)

$413

$1,615

2. Word Problems (Page 19)

a. $0.36 an hour

b. $1.75 an hour

3. Math Tools (Page 19)

$0.51

4. Math Notation (Page 20)

Some possible answers:

Pennies	Nickels	Dimes	Quarters	Half Dollars
1				1
1	10			
1		5		
1			2	
1	2	4		
1	1	2	1	
1	5		1	
1	4	3		

5. Open-Ended Problem (Page 20)

A. Do the Math

```
        80  patients per month
  ×   $100  per patient
  _____
     $8,000  per month

     $8,000
  −   1,800  assistant
  _____
     $6,200
  −   1,300  secretary
  _____
     $4,900
  −   1,700  rent
  _____
     $3,200  per month for Dr. Ting.
```

$3,200 x 12 = $38,400 for Dr. Ting per year.

1992

February
5 people did not pay x $100 = $500

April
15 people did not pay x $100 = $1,500

November
20 people did not pay x $100 = $2,000

$38,400
$$\begin{array}{r} \$38{,}400 \\ -\quad\ 500 \\ \hline \$37{,}900 \\ -\ 1{,}500 \\ \hline \$36{,}400 \\ -\ 2{,}000 \\ \hline \end{array}$$

$34,400 for Dr. Ting in 1992.

B. Do It Another Way (Page 21)

$$\begin{array}{r} 80 \ \text{patients per month} \\ \times\quad \$100 \ \text{per patient} \\ \hline \$8{,}000 \ \text{per month} \end{array}$$

$$\begin{array}{r} 1{,}800 \\ 1{,}300 \\ +\ 1{,}700 \\ \hline \$4{,}800 \end{array}$$

$$\begin{array}{r} \$8{,}000 \\ -\ 24{,}800 \\ \hline \$3{,}200 \end{array}$$

$3,200 x 12 = $38,400 for Dr. Ting per year.

$$\begin{array}{r} 1992 \\ 500 \\ 1{,}500 \\ +\ 2{,}000 \\ \hline \$4{,}000 \\ \$38{,}400 \\ -\quad 4{,}000 \\ \hline \$34{,}400 \ \text{in 1992} \end{array}$$

C. Let's Look At It

Dr. Ting
Dental Plan: $100/mo.

D. Explain the Math

Answers will vary, but should follow the student's choices in Section A.

First, I multiplied the number of patients by 100 to get the income for a month.

Then I subtracted the rent, assistant's pay, and secretary's pay. The doctor's monthly pay is $3,200.

Next, I multiplied the doctor's monthly pay by 12 to get her total yearly pay, $38,400.

After that, I multiplied the number of people who didn't pay in 1992, 40, by $100. 40 x $100 = $4,000.

Finally, I subtracted the missing money from $38,400 to get Dr. Ting's total for 1992.

E. Write the Answer

$3,200 / month
$38,400 / year
$34,400 in 1992

LESSON 6: OLYMPIC GAMES
1A. Mental Math (Page 22)

Olympic Games	Record	Olympic Games	Record
1st	25'	6th	26' 3"
2nd	25' 3"	7th	26' 6"
3rd	25' 6"	8th	26' 9"
4th	25' 9"	9th	27'
5th	26'	10th	27' 3"

1B. Pencil and Paper Math (Page 22)

7 min. 40 sec.   12 min. 2 sec.

13 min. 28 sec.   15 min. 49 sec.

29 min. 28 sec.   41 min. 1 sec.

1C. Calculator Math (Page 23)

1. 1,015.3   6. 825

2. 1,001   7. 748

3. 935   8. 753.5

4. 907.5   9. 643.5

5. 830.5   10. 594

5. Open-Ended Problem (Page 24)

A. Do the Math

$$\begin{array}{r} 2064 \\ -\ 2000 \\ \hline 64 \ \text{years} \end{array}$$

17 total number of Olympic Games
48 seconds = Record in the year 1996
17 Olympic Games x 1 second each − 17 seconds
faster
48 − 17 = 31 seconds

B. Do It Another Way

Olympic Year	Time	Olympic Year	Time
2000	47	2036	38
2004	46	2040	37
2008	45	2044	36
2012	44	2048	35
2016	43	2052	34
2020	42	2056	33
2024	41	2060	32
2028	40	2064	31
2032	39		

C. Let's Look At It

1 Sec. Faster/ Olympic Games

D. Explain the Math (Page 25)
First, I found the total number of years.
Then I found the total number of Olympic games in 64 years.
Next, I multiplied 17 by 1 to get the total number of seconds that the record will have decreased.
After that, I subtracted 17 from 48 (the record in 1996) to get the record in 2064.
Finally, I checked my answer by making a chart.

E. Write the Answer (Page 25)

31 seconds

LESSON 7: THE NEW DEAL: THE WORKS PROGRESS ADMINISTRATION

1A. Mental Math (Page 26)

1,000	700
800	1,250
700	276

1B. Pencil and Paper Math (Page 26)

300

301

1,300

1,301

11,404

15,505

Twenty thousand, two hundred two

Thirty thousand, three hundred three

Seventeen thousand, seven hundred seventeen

Six thousand, six hundred six

Eight thousand, eight hundred eighty

1C. Calculator Math (Page 27)

50,505	48,020
26,909	15,486
2,601	

2. Word Problems (Page 27)

a. 6

b. 40

c. $250,000

5. Open-Ended Problem (Page 28)

A. Do the Math

$$
\begin{array}{r}
120 \text{ dolls per month} \\
\times \quad 12 \text{ months a year} \\
\hline
1,440 \text{ dolls per year}
\end{array}
$$

1938 1939 1940 1941 1942 1943 = 6 years

$$
\begin{array}{r}
1,440 \text{ dolls} \\
\times \quad 6 \text{ years} \\
\hline
8,640 \text{ dolls from 1938–1943}
\end{array}
$$

B. Do It Another Way

Year	Dolls	Total
1938	1,440	1,440
1939	1,440	2,880
1940	1,440	4,320
1941	1,440	5,760
1942	1,440	7,200
1943	1,440	8,640

C. Let's Look At It

125/mo.
1935–1943

D. Explain the Math (Page 29)
Answers will vary, but should follow the student's choices in Section A.
First, I multiplied 120 (the number of dolls per month) by 12 to get 1,440 (the number of dolls per year).
Then I counted the years from 1938 to 1943 to get the total number of years.
Next, I multiplied 1440 by 6 to get the total number of dolls produced in the six year period.
Finally, I made a chart and checked my answer by adding.

E. Write the Answer

> 1,440 dolls / yr.
> 8,640 dolls from 1938 to 1943.

LESSON 8: DUCK® TAPE

1A. Mental Math (Page 30)
50,000

6,000

140

1B. Pencil and Paper Math (Page 30)

350	210	430
+ 430	+ 330	+ 530
780	540	960

640	400
+ 820	+ 480
1460	880

1C. Calculator Math (Page 30)
411   912   235,765

5,564,272   11,762,000

2. Word Problems (Page 31)
a. 2 rolls

b. 148 rolls

5. Open-Ended Problem (Page 31)
A. Do the Math
1000 ÷ 165 = 6.06
7 rolls

B. Do It Another Way (Page 32)

Rolls	Total Feet
1	165
2	330
3	495
4	660
5	825
6	990
7	1,155

C. Let's Look At It

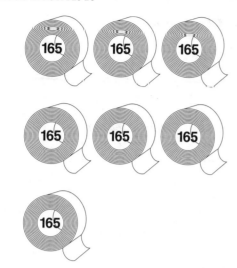

$$\begin{array}{r} 165 \\ \times \quad 7 \\ \hline 1{,}155 \end{array}$$

D. Explain the Math
First, I decided to use division, then check with addition.
Then I divided 1,000 feet by 165.
$1{,}000 \div 165 = 6.06$
Next, I saw that you cannot buy .06 roll.
After that, I rounded up to the next whole roll.
Finally, I checked my answer with addition. I made a chart and added 165 until I got more than 1,000.
$165 + 165 + 165 + 165 + 165 + 165 + 165 = 1{,}155.$

E. Write the Answer

7 rolls of tape

LESSON 9: THE UNITED STATES AUTO INDUSTRY

1A. Mental Math (Page 33)
46"   48"   66"

43"   56"   45"

1B. Pencil and Paper Math (Page 33)
$36'' + 36'' + 14'' = 86''$ $36'' + 36'' + 7'' = 79''$

$36'' + 29'' = 65''$ $36'' + 36'' + 36'' + 15'' = 123''$

$36'' + 36'' + 35'' = 107''$

1C. Calculator Math (Page 33)
76"   94"

132"   163"

106"

2. Word Problems (Page 34)
a. $4,087 more

b. 25 weeks

5. Open-Ended Problem (Page 34)
A. Do the Math

$35,000 x 11 = $385,000
$16,000 x 23 = $368,000
$385,000 − 368,000 = $17,000

B. Do It Another Way (Page 35)

$$\begin{array}{r} \$35{,}000 \text{ / car, Big Autos} \\ -\quad 16{,}000 \text{ / car, Compact Cars} \\ \hline \$19{,}000 \end{array}$$

$19,000 x 11 cars = $209,000

$$\begin{array}{r} 23 \\ -\quad 11 \text{ / mo.} \\ \hline 12 \text{ cars} \end{array}$$

12 cars x $16,000 = $192,000

209,000 − $192,000 = $17,000

C. Let's Look At It

$35,000
11/Mo.

$16,000
23/Mo.

D. Explain the Math

First, I decided to use multiplication, then subtraction.

Then I multiplied the number of cars for Big Autos by the price for each car to get the total amount of money Big Auto earned in a month.

Next, I multiplied the number of cars for Compact Cars by the price for each car to get the total amount of money Compact Cars earned in a month.

After that, I subtracted the total amount for Compact Cars from the total amount for Big Autos to find the difference.

Finally, I checked my answer by finding the price difference by car.

E. Write the Answer (Page 35)

> Big Autos, $17,000 more

LESSON 10: WAREHOUSE RETAIL STORES

1A. Mental Math (Page 36)

30	500	100
6500	100	70

1B. Pencil and Paper Math (Page 36)

300

1,300

11,300

111,300

four hundred

two thousand, four hundred

twelve thousand, four hundred

one hundred twelve thousand, four hundred

1C. Calculator Math (Page 37)

| 320,330 | 241,320 | 585,400 | 4,789,539 |

2. Word Problems

a. 18,150 items

b. 15,950 items

c. The city store, 1,500 more items

5. Open-Ended Problem (Page 38)

A. Do the Math

584 + 32 = 616

125,000 ÷ 616 = approximately 203 people per store

1,000 stores x 203 would be approximately 203,000 people

B. Do It Another Way

584 + 32 = 616

$$\frac{125,000}{616} = \frac{?}{1,000}$$

$$616 \text{ x } ? = 125,000,000$$

$$? = \frac{125,000,000}{616}$$

$$? = 203,000$$

C. Let's Look At It

Going to work...

203 people

D. Explain the Math (Page 39)

First, I read the problem and decided to add, then divide and multiply.

Then I added 584 to 32 to get the number of stores Home Depot had in 1998.

Next, I divided 125,000 by the number of stores to get an average number of people working in each store.

After that, I multiplied the number of people who worked in each store by 1,000.

Finally, I checked my answer by setting up a ratio.

E. Write the Answer

> 203,000 people

LESSON 11: OIL SPILLS

1A. Mental Math (Page 40)

6 quarts   9 quarts
1 gallon   3 gallons
8 quarts   13 quarts
2 gallons   8 quarts or 2 gallons: They are equal.

1B. Pencil and Paper Math (Page 41)

528

1,124

1,560

2,048

3,380

5,024

13,912

1C. Calculator Math (Page 41)

800	1,536
2,976	3,680
9,056	10,016
14,400	16,224

2. Word Problems (Page 41)

a. Tanker A, 750 gallons or 3,000 quarts
b. The people who poured oil down the drain, 7,500 gallons or 30,000 quarts
c. 3 quarts and 3 cups

4. Math Notation (Page 42)

How many—	
cups in a quart?	4
cups in a gallon?	16
tablespoons in a cup?	8
tablespoons in a quart?	32
tablespoons in a gallon?	128
teaspoons in a tablespoon?	3
teaspoons in a cup?	24
teaspoons in a quart?	96

5. Open-Ended Problem (Page 42)

A. Do the Math
1 gallon = 16 cups
8 ounces = 1 cup

     1 cup   lemonade
+   4 cups   water
_____

     5 cups
16 cups > 5 cups

B. Do It Another Way
1 gallon = 16 cups   1 cup = 8 ounces

   16 cups
−   4 cups of water
_____

   12 cups
−   1 cup mix
_____

   11 cups left

C. Let's Look At It

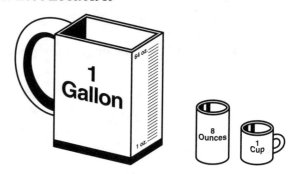

D. Explain the Math
Suggested Answer:
Answers will vary, but should follow the student's choices in Section A.
First I decided to convert all measurements to cups.
Then I converted the gallon jug to 16 cups.
Next, I converted the 8 ounces to 1 cup.
After that, I added the 1 cup of mix to the 4 cups of water. 1 + 4 = 5
Finally, I saw that the jug holds 16 cups. I need to make 5 cups. 16 > 5. I can make the lemonade in a gallon jug.

E. Write the Answer (Page 43)

yes

LESSON 12: DOES THE SUN EVER SET ON THE DISNEY EMPIRE?

1A. Mental Math (Page 45)

When it is ___ in Anaheim,	it is ___ in Orlando
1:00 A.M.	4:00 A.M.
2:00 A.M.	5:00 A.M.
3:00 A.M.	6:00 A.M.
4:00 A.M.	7:00 A.M.
5:00 A.M.	8:00 A.M.
6:00 A.M.	9:00 A.M.
7:00 A.M.	10:00 A.M.
8:00 A.M.	11:00 A.M.
9:00 A.M.	12:00 A.M.
10:00 A.M.	1:00 P.M.
11:00 A.M.	2:00 P.M.
12:00 A.M.	3:00 P.M.

1B. Pencil and Paper Math (Page 45)

six o'clock	six thirty
seven o'clock	seven thirty
nine o'clock	nine thirty
eleven o'clock	eleven thirty
twelve o'clock	twelve thirty
three o'clock	three thirty

1C. Calculator Math (Page 46)

24,000,000

24,300,000

415,800

2,421,825

7,260,470

2. Word Problems (Page 46)

a. 11:00 A.M.

b. 9:00 A.M.

c. 11:00 A.M.

4. Math Notation (Page 46)

Time Zone Chart

Here are some possible answers:

Anaheim	Orlando (+3)	Paris (+9)	Tokyo (+17)
1:00 A.M.	4:00 A.M.	10:00 A.M.	6:00 P.M.
3:00 A.M.	6:00 A.M.	12:00 P.M.	8:00 P.M.
5:00 A.M.	8:00 A.M.	2:00 P.M.	10:00 P.M.
7:00 A.M.	10:00 A.M.	4:00 P.M.	12:00 A.M.
9:00 A.M.	12:00 P.M.	6:00 P.M.	2:00 A.M.
12:00 P.M.	3:00 P.M.	9:00 P.M.	5:00 A.M.
2:00 P.M.	5:00 P.M.	11:00 P.M.	7:00 A.M.
4:00 P.M.	7:00 P.M.	1:00 A.M.	9:00 A.M.
6:00 P.M.	9:00 P.M.	3:00 A.M.	11:00 A.M.

5. Open-Ended Problem (Page 47)

A. Do the Math

Answers will vary depending on time specified for lunch. Some students will factor in time it takes to get from one ride to another.

7 rides x 8 minutes = 56 min.
7 rides x 45 minute wait for each = 315 min.
Lunch = 60 min.
Maximum time = 431 min.
431 ÷ 60 = 7 hrs., 11 min.

7 rides x 3 minute wait for each = 21 min.
Minimum time = 137 min.
137 ÷ 60 = 2 hrs., 17 min.

B. Do It Another Way (Page 48)

Suppose I arrive at 12:00 p.m.

	3 minute wait	45 minute wait
1st ride over at	12:11	12:53
2nd ride over at	12:22	1:46
etc.		

C. Let's Look At It

Ride Time (min.)	Wait Time	Lunch Time	Walk from Ride to Ride
56	3 x 7	45	3 x 7
56	45 x 7	45	3 x 7

D. Explain the Math
First, I calculated the amount of time spent on the rides (56 minutes).
Then I calculated the time spent waiting, if each ride had a 45-minute wait (315 minutes).
Next, I added 60 minutes for lunch.
After that, I calculated the time spent waiting, if each ride had a 3-minute wait (21 minutes)
Finally, I checked my answers with addition.

E. Write the Answer

> Between 2 hours, 17 minutes
> and 7 hours, 11 minutes

LESSON 13: IBM PLAYS CHESS

1A. Mental Math (Page 49)

$1 + 1 = 2$	$2 + 2 = 4$	$4 + 3 = 7$
$7 + 4 = 11$	$11 + 5 = 16$	$16 + 6 = 22$
$22 + 7 = 29$	$29 + 8 = 37$	$37 + 9 = 46$
$46 + 10 = 56$	$56 + 11 = 67$	$67 + 12 = 79$

1B. Pencil and Paper Math

$1 + 1 = 2$	$2 + 2 = 4$	$4 + 4 = 8$
$8 + 8 = 16$	$16 + 16 = 32$	$32 + 32 = 64$
$64 + 64 = 128$		

1C. Calculator Math

$1 \times 1 = 1$	$1 \times 2 = 2$	$2 \times 3 = 6$
$6 \times 4 = 24$	$24 \times 5 = 120$	$120 \times 6 = 720$
$720 \times 7 = 5,040$		

2. Word Problems (Page 50)

a. Mary – Michael – Cyndy

b. Mary – Cyndy – Michael

c. Michael – Cyndy – Mary

4. Math Notation
Each pawn, one or two spaces; each knight, 2 possibilities

5. Open-Ended Problem
A. Do the Math

	Wendy	Toshi	Sylvia	Jorge
Wendy				
Toshi	√			
Sylvia	√	√		
Jorge	√	√	√	

4 people will play 6 games
8 people will play 28 games

B. Do It Another Way (Page 51)

People	Games	I added
2	1	
3	3	2
4	6	3
5	10	4
6	15	5
7	21	6
8	28	7

C. Let's Look At It

	A	B	C	D	E	F	G	H
A								
B	√							
C	√	√						
D	√	√	√					
E	√	√	√	√				
F	√	√	√	√	√			
G	√	√	√	√	√	√		
H	√	√	√	√	√	√	√	

D. Explain the Math
First, I decided to make a chart.
Then, I put 8 people on the X axis and 8 people on the Y axis.
Next, I marked each game with a check (√).
After that, I saw a pattern.
Finally, I counted the games and checked my answer with the pattern.

E. Write the Answer

> 6 games / week
> 28 games / week

LESSON 14: TOPIC FOR THE 90S: GLOBAL WARMING

1A. Mental Math (Page 52)
72° F + 3° F = 75° F   37° F + 12° F = 49° F
15° F + 6° F = 21° F   68° F – 4° F = 64° F
102° F – 7° F = 95° F   51° F – 13° F = 38° F

1B. Pencil and Paper Math
  98° F   64° F   39° F
  34° F   103° F   111° F

1C. Calculator Math
125° F – 23° F = 102° F   118° F – 23°F = 95° F
109° F – 23° F = 86° F   91° F – 23° F = 68° F
70° F – 23° F = 47° F   48° F – 23° F = 25° F

2. Word Problems
January 42° F   May 75° F   September 79° F
February 44° F   June 84° F   October 69° F
March 52° F   July 88° F   November 56° F
April 65° F   August 86° F   December 44° F

5. Open-Ended Problem (Page 55)
A. Do the Math

41°									
40°									
39°									
38°									•
37°	•				•				
36°			•				•		
35°									
34°				•			•		
33°									
32°	•								
31°					•				•
30°									
1950 1955 1960 1965 1970 1975 1980 1985 1990 1995									

C. Let's Look At It

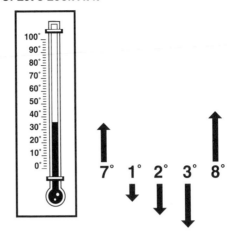

D. Explain the Math
First, I looked for a pattern.
Then I saw this pattern:
+5
–1
–2
–3
+6
–1
–2
–3
+7

Next, I used the pattern to find the temperatures.

1995	2000	2005	2010	2015	2020	2025	2030	2035	2040	2045	2050
38°	37°	35°	32°	40°	39°	38°	35°	44°	43°	41°	38°
+7	-1	-2	-3	+8	-1	-2	-3	+9	-1	-2	-3

After that, I circled the answers.
Finally, I checked my answers by making a graph.

E. Write the Answer

2030: 35°	2040: 43°	2050: 38°
2035: 44°	2045: 41°	

LESSON 15: "AS THE CROW FLIES"— OUR NATIONAL PARKS

1A. Mental Math (Page 57)

21years	7 years	8 years
11 years	8 years	

1B. Pencil and Paper Math (Page 57)

500,000
1,500,000
2,500,000
four million, five hundred thousand
five million, five hundred thousand
six million, five hundred thousand

1C. Calculator Math (Page 58)

5,952

3,425

5,652

792

11, 651

2. Word Problems

a. Denver to Miami, 630 miles longer
b. St. Louis to New York City, 56 miles shorter

4. Math Notation

Answers will vary depending on the size of the globe, and where a student positions the string on a state or country. They might run the string from capital to capital.

5. Open-Ended Problem (Page 59)

A. Do the Math

Starting Points	Virgin Islands National Park	Denali National Park	Olympic National Park	Canyonlands National Park	Guadalupe Mountains National Park
Peru	√				
Thailand		√			
Bangladesh		√			
California				√	√
England		√			
		Closest Park			

C. Let's Look At It (Page 60)

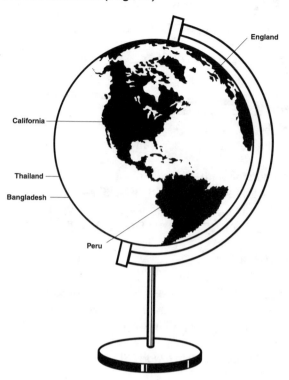

D. Explain the Math

First, I decided to chart the parks and the starting points.
Then I made the chart for the closest park.
Next I made the charts for the 2 closest parks.
After that, I used a string on a globe to fill in the charts.
Finally, I picked two parks because it depends on the starting points. For example, some places in California are closer to Utah, and some are closer to Washington.

E. Write the Answer

Denali National Park and
Olympic National Park
(because they are the closest parks for
the greatest number of people)

BUILDING READING SKILLS FOR SOCIAL STUDIES

INTRODUCTION

For the first three or four years of schooling, students learn to read. From grade four on, students read to learn. A student who has a strong foundation in reading by grade four will be able to handle the mainstream academic program. Reading ability is a good predictor of school success.

Unfortunately, many students read below grade level by grade four. In the United States there are more than one hundred programs that attempt to prevent or remediate reading failure. Two examples are "Reading Recovery" and CELL (California Early Literacy Learning). Designers of these programs want to assure that students are capable readers by grade four. By targeting weak readers with intense daily one-on-one tutoring, they advocate personal attention for their client schools' most academically fragile learners.

Some students have benefited from "crib time" and "lap time," terms that refer to a nurturing caregiver and the infant or toddler who spend hours and hours together sharing literature. Many students have not had this opportunity. Middle school and junior high classrooms include learners who have not learned how to read. Yet they are expected to use mainstream textbooks and keep pace with classmates who are proficient readers.

Other students enter schools with no prior education in English. Some have no prior education at all! So, in a single classroom, you might have very capable readers, reluctant readers, and nonreaders. Meeting state standards and designing a quality, high-level social studies curriculum depend on selecting materials that are accessible to all students. The grade level textbook overwhelms inefficient readers and nonreaders. Their response may be to put their heads down on their desks, draw pictures, or misbehave.

In *Building Reading Skills for Social Studies,* learners complete a variety of activities presented in alternating lesson formats. These activities develop reading skills as they provide content area information. Even students with no prior education can participate in the map and diagram activities.

HOW TO USE THIS BOOK

Each odd-numbered lesson has eleven sections:

1. Focus Question(s)

2. Vocabulary/Reference Skills

3. Reading

4. Skimming for Information

   Lessons 1 and 11: Complete a tabulation activity.

   Lessons 3, 5, 7, and 9: Complete a matching activity.

5. Literal Comprehension

   Lesson 1: Name the president.

   Lesson 3: Select the correct answer.

   Lessons 5 and 7: Indicate whether an answer is true or false.

   Lesson 9: Locate a date.

   Lesson 11: Name the orchestra.

6. Sequencing

7. Paraphrasing

8. Inferential Comprehension

9. Reference Skills

   Lesson 1: Use the phone book.

   Lesson 3: Consult encyclopedias and the Internet.

   Lesson 5: Get information from the "Yellow Pages."

   Lesson 7: Use an atlas.

   Lesson 9: Consult a dictionary.

   Lesson 11: Find information on the Internet.

10. Map Skills or Graphic Organizers

    Lessons 1, 9, and 11: Practice map skills.

    Lessons 3 and 5: Complete graphic organizers.

    Lesson 7: Graphing

11. Evaluative Comprehension

Each even-numbered lesson has six sections:

1. Focus Question(s)

2. Vocabulary/Reference Skills

3. Reading

4. Reading Rate

5. Illustrating Text

6. Following Written Instructions

While it is true that extensive reading can make better readers, it is not true that students learn how to read by reading a lot. Students must be taught how to read. In many settings this happens quite naturally as they are read to daily by family members and caregivers. For older learners with insufficient prior schooling, the reading process must be taught vigorously and systematically. These learners need a lot of exposure to the various skills that are required for reading comprehension.

How can we provide good reading instruction? First, students need time. They must devote enough time to the activities in this book so that they begin to master the skills that are required to manage the more complicated reading they will find in the general education textbooks. Students also need time to read alone. Books from the classroom library, the school library, or the community library should be available. These should be easy reading books about the topics of each lesson. They can be placed in baskets around the room, where students might have constant, easy access to them.

Second, we teachers must model how efficient readers approach passages and analyze them to find meaning. An important part of this modeling is showing students how to cite evidence to support an answer. We help them locate this evidence in the text.

Third, the content of the reading must be important. It should relate to something the students need to know. Especially for students with insufficient prior education, we must provide reading that assists them as they attempt to catch up to the general education students.

Fourth, as classrooms become more and more learner centered, students may work in pairs or groups to complete activities. Partnerships that develop among students often lead to additional activities that enhance learning. Moreover, teamwork has become a highly valued feature in the workplace.

EXTENSION ACTIVITIES

Lesson 1 Presidents from 1953 to 1981
- Students look at a state or national map. They find the interstate highways. On a local map, they find the closest major roads to where they are.

- Bring an illustrated book about astronauts to the classroom. Read it or talk about it with the students. Show a video of a space flight.

- Students use an encyclopedia to learn what the presidents' home states were. Then they put the presidents' names on their home states on an outline map of the United States.

- Students select one president from the lesson and find out more about him on the Internet.

Lesson 2 Cars

- Bring large toy cars to class for students to describe the parts of the cars. Students may draw one of the cars and label all the parts.

- Visit a local factory where something is manufactured. Guide students as they answer questions about the visit. Examples: What do they make at _____? How many people work there? What hours is the factory open?

- Bring a small object from home. Tell where and when it was invented. Students then bring something from home and learn how to find out where and when it was invented.

- Scan the text for the names of all the places mentioned in this lesson. Students highlight the places in the book and write them on an outline map.

Lesson 3 The Great Depression

- Students study the credit card offers we receive by mail. Point out the charges. Students search for the credit-card-issuing companies on the Internet.

- Students write and answer questions such as this one:

    A family needs clothes and a radio. They can spend $800. Describe the family. What do they buy? Why?

Item	Price	Item	Price
Radio	$65.00	Dress	$20.00
Jeans	$25.00	T-shirt	$10.00
Shoes	$20.00	Sweatshirt	$20.00

Much information is missing. Students work in teams to describe the family, the weather, and what clothes are needed. Then they make a shopping list and explain each purchase.

- Students find someone who remembers the Great Depression or a difficult economic situation in another country. They ask them to talk about it to the class, or to answer questions at an interview. Students may get the subject's permission to tape the interview for the class.

- Take the class to an auto dealership. Inquire what percentage of cars sell for cash and what percentage sell on credit. A salesperson can explain the different ways people buy and lease cars.

Lesson 4 : Earthquakes

- Ask students who have experienced earthquakes to illustrate, write about, or describe the event.

- Locate these places on a globe and map(s) with the students: In Alaska, Andreanof Islands, Cape Providence, Kodiak Island, Prince William Sound, Shumagin Islands; in California, Kern County, Northridge, San Francisco; and in Nevada, Pleasant Valley.

- Stage an earthquake drill in the classroom.

- Students find one additional historical fact for each year in which this lesson mentions an earthquake: 1900, 1903, 1906, 1938, 1952, 1957, 1964, and 1994.

Lesson 5 Organizations

- Students find the local YMCA in the phone book and locate it on a map. Take a field trip to the nearest YMCA. Arrange for a staff member to review the history of the organization.

- With students, find information on the YMCA or another similar organization on the Internet.

- Organize intramural chess, basketball, etc.

- Students graph YMCA expansion from data they obtain from the organization. They can get the information they need either by visiting a branch of the YMCA, by mail, or on the Internet.

Lesson 6 Computers

- Take students on a tour of the school to find where computers are located if there are few computers, or if they are all centrally located. If your school has many computers, have students try to find areas in which there are no computers.

- Organize computer versus low-tech races. One team types a passage while another team writes it. One team searches for information in an encyclopedia on disk while another locates the same information in the book format of an encyclopedia.

- Invite a telecommuter to class. Students might prepare questions to ask this worker.

- Have students make phone calls to inquire where people who have no computer may use one. They should phone photocopy stores, libraries, and local schools. After completing this assignment, they can report what they have learned to the class.

Lesson 7 Immigration

- Invite an immigration lawyer to class to answer questions that the students have prepared about immigration.

- Take a field trip to the local I&NS (Immigration and Naturalization Service) offices to learn what they do.

- If there are people where you live who have come from another place, locate on maps and a globe the routes they traveled from their homeland to where you are.

- Watch a TV show broadcast in another language.

Lesson 8 Recycling

- Guide students as they organize a recycling project in the classroom or school.

- In teams, students find a product to recycle. They describe how to recycle it and present their solution. Some ideas: flat soda pop cans, mesh citrus fruit bags, empty toothpaste tubes.

- As a service project, students arrange to visit a secondhand store and repair or refurbish donated toys and other items for resale.
- Students report on what energy sources are used in their homes and in other buildings they visit, such as markets, libraries and houses of worship.

Lesson 9 The Boston Marathon

- Students practice aural comprehension by calling local runners' hotlines and listening to recorded messages.
- They compose a letter to the nearest marathon organization to obtain a map of the marathon.
- Guide students as they design and map a short course near the school.
- Invite a physician to class to show how running affects cardiovascular fitness.

Lesson 10 Four Modern Conveniences

- Students interview one another and create a table of the class's preferred writing implements.

There should be different types of pens and pencils listed on the chart.

Student's Name	Preferred Writing Implement
_____	_____
_____	_____
_____	_____

- Initiate a conversation about neon signs and painted signs. Where should each be used? Why?
- Organize a taste test of identical foods prepared in a microwave and in a conventional oven. Display the results.

TASTE TEST

Student	Food	Preference Microwave	Conventional
_____	_____	_____	_____
_____	_____	_____	_____
_____	_____	_____	_____

- To clarify and improve vocabulary, demonstrate different visual media: drawings, photographs, movies, videos, and computer-generated art.

Lesson 11 Music: Six Orchestras

- Provide background audio or video of a local orchestra performance.
- Guide students as they search for orchestras on the Internet. They can enter the name of a city and the words *orchestra, symphony,* or *philharmonic.*

- To improve wide reading, have students bring the Sunday paper to class. Search for listings of orchestra events.

- Invite a music teacher to demonstrate instruments of the orchestra to the class.

Lesson 12 Conflicts: World War II

- Locate Allies and Axis countries on a globe.

- Invite a member of the National Guard to the class to discuss the organization's role in maintaining peace.

- Invite a school counselor to the class to talk about resolving conflicts.

- Students look in the daily papers for information about current conflicts throughout the world. Then they locate the locations of the conflicts on maps or on a globe.

ANSWER KEY: BUILDING READING SKILLS FOR SOCIAL STUDIES

Answers are given where they are definitive. In many instances answers will vary. The integrated feature of the series means students will derive unique answers depending on how they respond to the questions.

LESSON 1: PRESIDENTS FROM 1953 TO 1981

Focus Question (Page 1)
Answers will vary from term to term.

Vocabulary/Reference Skills (Page 1)

astronaut: a pilot or crew member on a spaceship

concert: a musical performance

health: being well or not sick

highway: a main road

peace: freedom from war

poverty: being poor, having no money

ship: a big boat

space: the room or place all around the earth and beyond our solar system

visit: go to see

war: fighting by armies between countries or parts of countries; the opposite of peace

Skimming for Information (Page 2)

Carter, James E.	1977–1981
Eisenhower, Dwight D.	1953–1961
Ford, Gerald R.	1974–1977
Johnson, Lyndon B.	1963–1969
Kennedy, John F.	1961–1963
Nixon, Richard M.	1969–1974

Literal Comprehension (Page 2)

Dwight D. Eisenhower

James E. Carter

Lyndon B. Johnson

Gerald R. Ford

John F. Kennedy

Richard M. Nixon

Sequencing (Page 3)

1953–1961	Dwight D. Eisenhower
1961–1963	John F. Kennedy
1963–1969	Lyndon B. Johnson
1969–1974	Richard M. Nixon
1974–1977	Gerald R. Ford
1977–1981	James E. Carter

Paraphrasing (Page 3)
1. d
2. e
3. f
4. a
5. b
6. c

Inferential Comprehension (Page 3)

• Answer will vary from year to year.

• Israel and Egypt

• Longest: Eisenhower; shortest: Kennedy

• War on Poverty

Map Skills (Page 4)

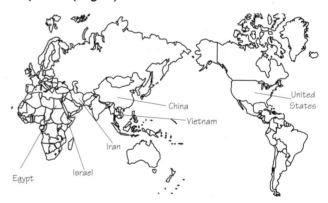

Evaluative Comprehension
Sample: Johnson— War on Poverty

LESSON 2: CARS

Vocabulary/Reference Skills (Page 5)

1. assembly line: a row of workers and machines. Work is passed along the row until a product is made.
2. automobile: a vehicle, a car
3. earn: make money
4. factory: a building or buildings where things are made
5. firm: company
6. industry: a kind of business
7. manufacture: make by hand or machine; the making of a product
8. vehicle: a means of carrying things or people such as a car, truck, or van

Reading (Pages 5–8)

A. 1
B. 3
C. 1. cost less.
D. 3. the cars cost less.
E. 1901   425 cars
    1902   3,750 cars
    1903   5,000 cars
F. *Ford only:* Henry Ford started it. He started it in Michigan.
   General Motors only: William C. Durant started it. He started it in Delaware.
   Ford and General Motors: big car companies; factories in Detroit; assembly lines
G. 1. Cars changed how people lived.
H. 1. good for the hotel industry.

LESSON 3: THE GREAT DEPRESSION

Vocabulary / Reference Skills (Page 10)

1. business: a store or factory
2. cash: money in the form of coins and bills
3. credit: belief that someone can and will pay later
4. Depression: a time when people do not have money
5. drop: fall; go lower
6. earnings: money received for work
7. great: very big
8. price: cost; amount of money to pay for things
9. produce: make, manufacture
10. salary: an amount of money paid for regular work
11. shop: visit stores to look for things to buy
12. unemployed: out of a job, without work

Skimming for Information (Page 11)

1. e
2. a
3. d
4. b
5. c

Literal Comprehension (Page 11)

1. did not get rich
2. did not have
3. many things
4. Many people
5. got smaller
6. Franklin D. Roosevelt

Sequencing (Page 12)

- People bought things on credit.
- Herbert Hoover was elected president.
- There was no more credit.
- Nine percent of the people could not find work.
- Franklin D. Roosevelt was elected president.

Paraphrasing (Page 12)

1. d
2. a
3. e
4. b
5. c
6. g
7. f

Inferential Comprehension (Page 12)

1933, because more people were out of work.

because they didn't have enough cash

because people were not buying things

They were unhappy with Hoover.

Reference Skills (Page 13)

Information can be found at home, at school, and at a community or university library. It can be found on the Internet, in encyclopedias such as *Encyclopedia Britannica, Colliers,* and *World Book,* and in other reference books such as dictionaries and atlases.

Graphic Organizer (Page 13)

Did Not Have Money	Had Some Money
They bought on credit.	He was rich.
He had no job.	She bought with cash.
They could not pay.	They bought a lot of clothes.
She was poor.	
They could not buy cars.	

Evaluative Comprehension (Page 14)

Sample answers: Buy now, pay later. You do not have to carry money. You buy what you cannot pay for.

LESSON 4: EARTHQUAKES

Focus Questions (Page 15)

1. Answers will vary.
2. Earthquakes happen in many places in the world. In the United States the greatest number of earthquakes have occurred in California and Alaska.

Vocabulary / Reference Skills (Page 15)

1. damage: hurt, harm, make worse
2. earth: ground
3. fewest: the smallest number of
4. ground: the surface of the earth; soil
5. harm: damage, hurt, destruction
6. higher: taller, farther up
7. hurt: harm, damage
8. measure: find out the size of something
9. move: change place or position, put or keep in motion
10. occur: happen
11. raise: lift, elevate
12. scale: a system used for measuring
13. shook: trembled, moved from side to side

Reading (Pages 16–18)

A. 2. Earthquakes can be measured.
B. 3. He lived in California.
C. 2. In 1935.
D. 2. burned for a long time.
E. 1. the earthquake broke water lines.
F. 1. Alaska has had very big earthquakes.
G. 2. 1915
H. 1. It was early in the morning.
I. 3. North Dakota and Florida
J. 1. Alaska
K. 1. AK, Alaska 2. CA, California 3. FL, Florida
   4. ND, North Dakota 5. NV, Nevada

Reading Rate (Page 19)

The Richter scale measures earthquakes. An earthquake can be very small. A small quake is a micro earthquake. Other quakes are stronger. These great earthquakes happen about once a year.

Quakes occur all over the world. Japan has many earthquakes. There are also quakes in Indonesia and Colombia. Where else are there earthquakes?

Illustrating Text (Page 19)

The three states are (from left to right) California, Nevada, and Alaska. Big quakes occurred in California in 1906, 1952, and 1994; in Nevada in 1915; and in Alaska in 1900, 1903, 1938, 1957, and 1964.

LESSON 5: ORGANIZATIONS

Vocabulary/Reference Skills (Page 20)

1. belonged: (belong: be part of) was a part of
2. camping: living away from home for a while in a tent
3. childcare: taking care of children
4. Depression: a time when people do not have money
5. during: through the time of, while or when
6. fitness: good condition of body and mind
7. growing: (grow: get bigger) getting bigger
8. hard: difficult
9. organization: a group of people who work together for a reason
10. run: manage, direct
11. summer camps: places to stay for a short time in the summer

Skimming for Information (Page 21)

1. e
2. a
3. f
4. b
5. c
6. d

Literal Comprehension (Page 21)

1. F
2. T
3. T
4. T
5. F
6. F

Sequencing (Page 22)

1. The YMCA begins in London.
2. The YMCA begins in the United States.
3. The YMCA starts summer camps.
4. The Great Depression
5. World War II
6. Much interest in fitness

Paraphrasing (Page 22)

1. e
2. f
3. b
4. c
5. d
6. a

Making Inferences (Page 22)

1. Answers will vary depending on the date.
2. It grew faster in Great Britain.
3. They can swim, play basketball and volleyball, and work out.
4. no; only for men

Reference Skills (Page 23)

Answers will vary for all questions.

Inferential Comprehension (Page 23)

1. a. It grew.
2. c. More people went to the YMCA.
3. a. YMCAs had gyms and pools.
4. b. childcare

Abbreviations / Reference Skills (Page 24)

1. Apr.—April
2. bldg.—building
3. DC—District of Columbia, the capital of the United States
4. EDT—eastern daylight time
5. FYI—for your information
6. kW—kilowatt
7. MD—Maryland
8. M.D.—medical doctor
9. mts.—mountains

Graphic Organizer (Page 24)

The YMCA grew bigger in the 1840s, 1850s, 1900s, 1950s, and 1980s. It did not grow a lot in the 1930s, 1960s, and 1970s (although people did become more interested in fitness in the 1970s).

Evaluative Comprehension (Page 24)

Most students will suggest that the YMCA is a good organizations because it provides a place to go, something to do, sports, camps, help, fitness, pools, gyms, and childcare.

LESSON 6: COMPUTERS

Vocabulary / Reference Skills (Page 25)

1. additional: extra, more
2. building: a thing that is built. Houses, schools, and stores are buildings.
3. computer: a machine that does some kinds of work quickly
4. design: make a plan for something
5. factory: a building or buildings where things are made
6. laptop: a small computer you can hold on your lap
7. office: a room or rooms where people work
8. report: a written account of something

Reading (Pages 26–28)

A. 2. ENIAC was the first computer.
B. 1. better than ENIAC.
C. 3. did not make computers on an assembly line.
D. 1. They were small.
E.

1983	IBM	IBM XT
1984	Apple	Macintosh
1985	Commodore	Amiga 1000

F. For Get Information and Contact Others check marks go in all three boxes. For Play Games check marks go in At Home and At School.
G. 2. There are many kinds of technology.
H. 1. to work away from the office.
I. at home, in hotels, on planes, and elsewhere

Some of the (IBM) (computers) are the (IBM) 701, the (IBM) 650 and the (IBM) System 360. (Apple) made the (Apple) IIC (computer,) the (Apple) IIE (computer) and the (Apple) Macintosh (computer.) Both (IBM) and (Apple) have made many (computers.) Many offices have (IBM) (computers,) and many schools have (Apple) (computers.)

LESSON 7: IMMIGRATION

Vocabulary / Reference Skills (Page 30)
1. homeland: a country that is a person's home
2. immigrant: a person who comes into another country to live
3. immigrate: to move to another country to live
4. immigration: movement of people from one country to another to live.
5. law: a rule made by a government
6. limit: restrict; keep down

Skimming for Information (Page 31)
1. d
2. e
3. c
4. a
5. b

Literal Comprehension (Page 31)
1. T
2. F
3. F
4. T
5. T

Sequencing (Page 32)
1. More than nine million people came here.
2. A law limited immigration.
3. More than 20,000 people came from Haiti.
4. More than 600,000 people came from Europe.

Paraphrasing (Page 32)
1. g
2. f
3. d
4. b
5. c
6. e
7. a

Inferential Comprehension (Page 32)
1. Yes. They can find better jobs here.
2. Before 1965 most immigrants came from Europe.
3. from the Americas.
4. Mexico, Haiti, the Dominican Republic, and Jamaica.

Reference Skills (Page 33)

Graphing (Page 33)

Evaluative Comprehension (Page 33)
People immigrate to the United States because they have families here, because they want to work here, and because they had to leave their homelands.

LESSON 8: RECYCLING

Focus Questions (Page 34)
1. Answers will vary.
2. Yes, depending on the strength of the bag
3. Sample answers: to hold groceries (and other products), to hold garbage, to package lunches, to protect things from dust and dirt.

Vocabulary / Reference Skills (Page 34)
1. award: prize
2. coal: a black mineral that burns
3. curbside: the side of the street near the curb
4. disposable: able to be thrown away after use
5. drop-off: leave at a place
6. gas: substance that is not a solid and not a liquid; substance that has no shape or size

7. industry: a kind of business
8. oil: a liquid that burns
9. pollution: making dirty
10. power: strength
11. recycle: use something over again; make useful things from waste
12. reuse: use again
13. waste: things that are left over or not used; things to be thrown away

Reading (Pages 35–37)
A. 3. Pollution is not new.
B. 1. making useful things from waste
C. 2. More people lived in cities.
D. 1st: You buy the can. 2nd: You use what is in the can. 3rd: You take the can back to the store. 4th: The can is cleaned. 5th: The can is reused.
E. Davis only: recycled newspapers
   Maplewood only: recycled leaves
   Davis and Maplewood: recycle bottles and cans; recycle many things; have won awards
F. 3. Recycling changed from drop-off to curbside.
G. 2. Newtown will have drop-off, then curbside recycling.

Reading Rate (Page 37)

Some people (recycle) more than others. They (collect) (recyclables) or put them out for (collection.) (Collection) happens two to four times a month. (Recycling) can be fun. It can be hard work, too. It takes a long time to (collect.) Although some people like to (recycle) others say (recycling) is not important. Today, most people (collect) and (recycle)

LESSON 9: THE BOSTON MARATHON

Vocabulary / Reference Skills (Page 39)
1. company: a group of people that does business
2. dusty: full of very small dirt particles
3. few: not many
4. go to: visit by computer on the Internet
5. Internet: a way to find information by using a computer
6. marathon: a foot race about 26 miles long
7. marathoner: a person who runs in a marathon
8. muddy: full of wet earth
9. overseas: across the sea or ocean
10. runner: a person who runs
11. winner: the person or thing who wins

Skimming for Information (Page 40)
1. b
2. f
3. d
4. c
5. e
6. a

Literal Comprehension (Page 41)
1. 1989–1995
2. 1952
3. 1951
4. 1980s
5. 1933, 1938, 1941
6. 1897

Sequencing (Page 41)
1. The Boston Marathon started.
2. A man from Finland won.
3. A big company helped the Boston Marathon.
4. A woman from Poland won.
5. The Boston Marathon was 100 years old.

Paraphrasing (Page 42)
1. h
2. c
3. e
4. a
5. d
6. f
7. b
8. g

Inferential Comprehension (Page 42)
1. b
2. a
3. a
4. c
5. c

Map Skills (Page 43)

Ann Arbor, Michigan
Michigan Trail

Boston, Massachusetts
Boston Marathon

Boise, Idaho
Great Potato

Sandy Hook, New Jersey
Jersey Shore

Amarillo, Texas
Lone Star
Paper Chase

Melbourne, Florida
Wickham Park Trail

1. Sample answer: It provides competition for runners. It provides entertainment for spectators.
2. Sample answer: The weather might be bad.

LESSON 10: FOUR MODERN CONVENIENCES

Vocabulary / Reference Skills (Page 44)

1. ballpoint pen: a pen that writes with a tiny hard ball at its tip
2. broadcast: send out by radio or TV
3. convenience: being easy
4. item: thing; object
5. microwave: an oven that cooks with electromagnetic waves instead of heat
6. modern: new, recent
7. neon: a gas
8. neon sign: a sign that is lighted with neon gas
9. patent: a license to own a product you invent
10. store: a place where things are for sale
11. VCR: videocassette recorder
12. wiring: a system of wires to carry electricity

Reading (Pages 45–47)

A. 3. Modern conveniences make life easier.
B. 2. John H. Loud
C. 3. Many ballpoint pens were sold in England.
D. 2. Pilots used to fly high.
E. 3. radio waves
F. b needed special wiring
G. 1940s: People began to make VCRs.
   1956: A video recording was made in California.
   1959: A smaller VCR was made in Japan.
   1970s: Most VCRs were sold in schools.
   1975: A VCR was made for home use.
H.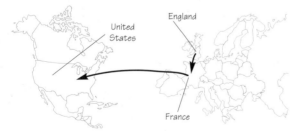

Reading Rate (Page 48)

I was watching my (VCR) when I heard the (microwave) beep. On the video there were ads for ball-point pens and (neon signs.) I shut off the (VCR) and pointed my car toward the (neon signs) store. They had (neon signs) for everything—(VCRs,) (microwaves,) ball-point pens, even (neon signs!)

LESSON 11: SIX ORCHESTRAS

Vocabulary / Reference Skills (Page 49)

1. appear: begin; come into being
2. concert: a musical performance
3. conductor: the leader of the orchestra
4. free: at no cost
5. listen: try to hear, pay attention
6. musician: a person who sings or plays music
7. orchestra: a group of musicians who play at a concert
8. perform: put on a show
9. philharmonic: having to do with music
10. recording: tape or disc used to hold sounds
11. symphony: orchestra

Skimming for Information (Page 50)

1900—Dallas Symphony Orchestra
1914—Detroit Symphony Orchestra
1919—Los Angeles Philharmonic
1922—New Jersey Symphony Orchestra
1930—Indianapolis Symphony Orchestra
1939—West Virginia Symphony Orchestra

Literal Comprehension (Page 51)

1. New Jersey Symphony and West Virginia Symphony
2. Los Angeles Philharmonic
3. Dallas Symphony
4. Indianapolis Symphony
5. New Jersey Symphony
6. West Virginia Symphony

Sequencing (Page 51)

1919	Los Angeles	It began.
1922	Detroit	It went on the radio.
1930	Indianapolis	It began.
1942	Dallas	Musicians served in World War II.
1942	West Virginia	The conductor left.
1960s	New Jersey	Many people learned about it.

Paraphrasing (Page 52)

1. d
2. c
3. a
4. e
5. b

Inferential Comprehension (Page 52)

1. c
2. c
3. a
4. c
5. a
6. b

Reference Skills (Page 53)

Dallas Symphony Orchestra
Detroit Symphony Orchestra
Los Angeles Philharmonic
New Jersey Symphony Orchestra
Indianapolis Symphony Orchestra
West Virginia Symphony Orchestra

Map Skills (Page 53)

1st row, left to right: Texas / Dallas Symphony
Orchestra; Michigan / Detroit Symphony
Orchestra; California / Los Angeles
Philharmonic

2nd row, left to right: New Jersey / New Jersey
Symphony Orchestra; Indiana / Indianapolis
Symphony Orchestra; West Virginia / West
Virginia Symphony Orchestra

Evaluative Comprehension (Page 53)

Sample answer: It entertains people. It makes
recordings. It gives free concerts.

LESSON 12: WORLD WAR II

Focus Questions (Page 54)

Answers will vary for both questions.

Vocabulary / Reference Skills (Page 54)

1. continent: one of the large land areas on the
   earth, such as South America or Africa
2. income: money for work
3. isolate: set apart, keep away
4. isolationists: people who don't want their
   country to be involved with other countries
5. peace: freedom from war
6. rose: went up
7. soldier: a person who serves in an army
8. tax: money paid to a government
9. trillion: one thousand billion

Reading (Pages 54–57)

A. Allies: Great Britain, the United States,
   Canada, China, France, the Soviet Union
   Axis: Germany, Italy, Japan
B. c. They wanted the United States to stay out of
   war.
C. b. seventy million
D. a. with ships
E. 3. Incomes rose.
F. Asia: China, Japan
   Europe: Belgium, France, Great Britain,
   Poland, the Soviet Union, Austria, Bulgaria,
   Finland, Germany, Hungary, Italy, and
   Rumania
   Oceania: Australia
   North America: the United States
   Axis: Austria, Bulgaria, Finland, Germany,
   Hungary, Italy, Romania, Japan
   Allies: Belgium, France, Great Britain, Poland,
   the Soviet Union, China, Australia
G. 1. b. Allies and Axis countries joined to form
   the UN.
   2. a. Winston Churchill was Prime Minister of
   the UN.
H. 1. c. in 1944
   2. c. with words

Reading Rate (Page 57)

The (conflict,) like all (conflicts,) forced a (war)
industry. (Wars) need goods and (soldiers.) Every
(soldier) going to (war) needs (war) materials. (Wars)
could be won by well equipped (soldiers) with
proper (conflict) gear. Training (soldiers) for
(conflicts) prepares them to go to (war.) Countries
could spend a lot of money on (wars) and (conflicts.)

Map Skills (Page 58)

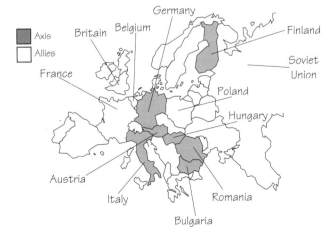

BUILDING SCIENCE SKILLS FOR SOCIAL STUDIES

INTRODUCTION

Several organizations are working to improve science education in the United States. Some of them are the American Association for the Advancement of Science (AAAS), the National Science Teachers Association, and the National Science Foundation. In the Fall/Winter 1997 volume of 2061 Today, F. James Rutherford, Director of the AAAS, calls for the reform of science education. He asks for "significant changes in that vast, complicated, and incredibly disaggregated non-system called American education."

The United States has no national science curriculum, however individual states are working to develop standards and benchmarks for science literacy. The AAAS encourages teachers to look at the success of science education abroad, where national standards drive the curriculum. Science literacy depends on giving students the chance to study the selected topics in depth. What they learn from this process they will be able to apply to other topics. Both process and content are important in science inquiry.

The AAAS, through Project 2061, targets science literacy as its goal. *Benchmarks for Science Literacy*, a document produced by Project 2061, is a statement of what science learning should take place during the different stages of K–12 education. It delineates the abilities that we are to help students develop at each level. Before entering high school, students should know how to:

- Ask questions.

- Make and organize collections.

- Make observations in and out of the science classroom setting.

- Describe science inquiry as a sequence that includes posing a question, collecting data, making and testing hypotheses, and figuring out how to respond to the question.

- Make presentations to clearly communicate results after gathering and recording them accurately.

- Work on a team, but make individual observations.

- Comprehend that there could be different results from repeated trials, and that good science means repeating experiments many times before formulating a conclusion.

- Seek evidence to support statements.

HOW TO USE THIS BOOK

Each of the 15 lessons in *Building Science Skills for Social Studies* derives from a social studies topic. Teachers may select the five lessons that most closely align to local and state curricula at their grade levels. When students complete these lessons, they will know the basic features of scientific inquiry, and they will be able to formulate and test hypotheses. Spending more time on fewer topics helps students learn the approach to scientific inquiry, an approach that will guide them to work efficiently with any science topics they study in the future.

Here is a list of the lessons in Building Science Skills for Social Studies.

EXTENSION ACTIVITIES

Although we want students to complete the lessons as written, the most important activity is what begins after each lesson. This is when students ask the "What if. . . ?" questions. As you work through this book, encourage students to ask questions. Each one of these questions can become an investigation in itself. When working on a lesson, keep a large piece of chart paper on the wall on which students can write the questions they have for further study.

This "Inquiry Wall" can become the jumping-off point for the next lesson. The teacher becomes the guide, not the solution. Science students get more excited about inquiries they design than about those they find in books. When it is they who have asked the questions, they become more aggressive investigators. If students have posed several questions for further study, they may group themselves in teams to design and carry out the project or investigation. Different groups of scientists often study the same question. This provides a set of checks and balances in the scientific community, and students may do likewise. If many students have signed up for a single inquiry, form small groups, and explain the importance of independent investigations.

Students can formulate inquiry questions by completing the following:

- Why does...?

- What is the reason for...?

- When do...?

- How many...?

Explaining science by themselves helps students make sense of it. In presentations to the class, each group should discuss its findings. This discussion should contain these features:

- Background information

- Data collection

- Record keeping

- Observations

- Evidence leading to a conclusion

Finally, young students will not learn all there is to learn about science by coming up with questions and experimenting to look for answers. Direct teaching of science concepts and extensive reading about successful scientists are essential components of the science program. However, students who know how to participate in scientific inquiry will prosper as they acquire scientific literacy.

ANSWER KEY, BUILDING SCIENCE SKILLS FOR SOCIAL STUDIES

Answers are given where they are definitive. In many instances answers will vary. The integrated feature of the series means students will derive unique answers depending on how they respond to the questions.

LESSON 1: ROCK ART

(Page 2)

(Page 4)

Observations

Answers will vary in chart based on other students' responses.

Students should state the <u>number</u> of people who got the message and the <u>number</u> of people who did not.

Conclusions

1. yes
2. Depends on student's opinion
3. Answers may vary but should imply a very long time

LESSON 2: RECYCLING

(Page 5)

Procedure

1. Answers will vary based on what object the student chooses.
2. Some possible answers are: PLASTIC TRAY:

part of a beekeeper's hat, paint and hang in a window, organize a drawer or a desk, store cookies or other food items, grow plants; ALUMINUM PIE PLATE: perforate and use as a planter, reheat leftovers, invert and make a hat. store cookies or other food item, make your own pie and use this plate, use under a plant to catch water; GLASS JAR: store pens and pencils, paper clips, or tacks, put a plant or flower in it, put iced tea or another drink in it, collect dirt, plants, and insects

(Page 6)

3. Answers will vary based on other students' responses.
4. Answers will vary based on what students choose to do with their objects.
5. First answer should be the object students chose on p 5, Procedure #1.
   Second answer should describe what student drew in #4 on p. 6.
6. Answer should be the object students chose on p. 5, Procedure #1.
7. Answers will vary based on students' projects.

(Page 8)

4. Answers should correspond to dates circled on chart, p. 7.
5. Answers will vary based on amount of paper collected.
6. Look of graph will depend on amount of paper collected. Each week, students should make a dot in the column for that week showing how many papers they counted. At the end of the 5 weeks, they should connect the dots to complete the graph.

LESSON 3: ACID RAIN

(Page 10)

Observation 1

1. Answer will be based on student observations during activity.
2. Answers will be based on student observations during activity.

(Page 11)

Observations 2

1. Answer will be based on student observations during activity.
2. Answers will be based on student observations during the activity.
3. Answers will vary, but should correspond to responses to questions 1 and 2 above.

Conclusions

Air moves; Blowing air moves; Blowing air moves faster than still air.

(Page 12)
Question
Answers will vary, but should be based on student observations during activity.

Conclusions
acidic; more; less; moves; more acidic

LESSON 4: DID YOU HEAR THE BELL?

(Page 14)
Observations
1. It sounds different, but it may sound the same to some students.
2. It sounds different than when my partner or I pluck it near the end. Answers will vary, however.

(Page 15)
3. I can hear my partner.

Conclusions
2. If the string is tight, sound travels along it.

(Page 16)
Observations
The sound is louder when my hands are on my head. Answers will vary, however.

Conclusions
Sound moving through my head is quieter.
Sound moving through air is louder.
With my hands on my head the sound is quieter.
With my hands off my head the sound is louder.

How Does This Sound?
Responses will vary depending on which inquiry interests the student.

LESSON 5: IT'S ABOUT TIME!

(Page 18)
Observations
1. Answers will vary based on geographic location.
2. Answers will vary based on geographic location.

(Page 19)
3. Answers will vary, but should correspond to answers in chart in Observations #2, p. 18.

Observation
It is not daytime everywhere. (Answers to remaining questions will vary based on geographic location and time of year.)

(Page 20)
Procedure
The places in the chart below are suggestions only.

Line of Longitude	Place	Place	Line of Longitude	Place	Place
0°	Greenwich, England	Reggane, Algeria	165°	Gizhig, Siberia Samarai,	Pam, New Caldonia
15°	Bissau, Guinea	Budir, Iceland	150°	Papua New Guinea	Eden, Australia
30°	Ljeskov, South Sandwich Islands South	Greenland Viana, Brazil South	135°	Iman, Siberia	Udskoye, Siberia
45°	Orkney Island	Shetland Islands	120°	Marble Bar, Australia	Taishun, China
60°	Goose Bay, Newfoundland	Prainha, Brazil	105°	Zhugqu, China	Yessey, Siberia
		Philadelphia, Pennsylvania	90°	Dacca, Bangladesh	Thimbu, Bhutan
75°	Ica, Peru	Campeche, Mexico	75°	Ajmer, India	Sri nangar, India
90°	Peter I Island				
105°	Boulder, Colorado	Alamogordo, New Mexico	60°	Mashhad, Iran	Mahot, Oman
120°	Santa Barbara California	Dawson Creek, Canada	45°	Ansalova. Madagascar	Thilisi, Georgia
135°	Sitka, Alaska	Gambier Island	30°	Krgali, Rwanda	Cairo, Egypt
		Bettles, Alaska	15°	Messina, Sicily	Tmassah, Libya
150°	Caroline	Dutch Harbor, Alaska			
165°	Nome, Alaska		0°	Accra, Ghana	Gao, Mali
180°	Uelkal, Siberia	Suva, Fiji			

Questions
Yes; 24; 15°

LESSON 6: GEORGE DID IT!

(Page 23)
Count the Peanuts
Answers will vary, but may include cookies, candy, Asian foods, cereals, breads, sauces, dressings, syrups; answers for the rest of the exercise will vary based on student ideas.

LESSON 7: WATERSHEDS

(Page 27)
Observations
Answers will vary depending on outcome of activity, but here are some probable answers:

	sod	soil
clear	X	
full of soil		X
full of grass		
blue		X
sudsy		X
oily		X

Conclusions
1. The water becomes dirty. Bad things go to the river or land.
2. The water is clean.

Take a Survey
Answers in this section will vary based on student opinions and results of surveys.

(Page 29)
Map Your Watershed
Answers will vary based on geographical location.

(Page 30)
Observation
The number of minutes, hours, days, depends on heat, humidity, seal on jar, moisture in soil, etc.

Conclusions
Arrows will show moisture collecting at the top and falling.

LESSON 8: THE CAR AND THE ASSEMBLY LINE

(Page 34)
Conclusions
Answers will vary based on class performance, but the answer to question 3 will usually be to have one person do all the work.

faster; more; faster; work gets done more quickly and no step is forgotten; people don't develop as many skills and don't have the satisfaction of creating an entire product; probably

LESSON 9: WHAT SIZE IS YOUR PARACHUTE?

(Page 37)
Observations
All answers will vary based on what type of parachute students choose to build, how carefully they construct it, and the results of the activity.

(Page 38)
Conclusions
Students' conclusions will depend on their parachute experiments.

Observation
The hole usually makes the parachute fall faster.

Conclusions
Students' combinations determine the results; even students following the same procedure get different results.

LESSON 10: THE DUST BOWL AND EROSION

(Page 40)
Observations
Dry, loose soil will blow out of the pan.
Drawings will vary based on results of activity.

Conclusions
1. plants and water
2. soil without plants; dry soil

LESSON 11: LET'S JET AWAY!

(Page 43)
Observations
1. Answers will vary based on results of activity (inflation, size of release hole, etc.)
2. Long balloons go faster than round balloons. Small balloons go faster than big balloons. Long balloons go farther than round balloons. Small balloons go farther than big balloons. Big balloons have more air to escape. The air goes out the back of the balloon. The balloon goes forward.

Try it on water!
Answers in this section will vary based on what experiment students decide to do.

LESSON 12: BUILDING BRIDGES

(Page 46)

Observations
Answer depends on outcome of step 1 of this section.

Conclusions
Answers will vary, but things that cross bridges can include: animals, trucks, people, and bicycles. Answers to remaining questions in this section will vary based on results of activity.

(Page 48)

Do the Math
Answers will vary based on how students chose to construct bridges.

Bridge Comparison
Answers will vary based on results of activity.

LESSON 13: TOOLS FOR INFORMATION

(Page 51)

Procedure
Answers will vary based on results of activity.

(Page 52)

Observations
Answers will vary based on results of activity.

LESSON 14: THE WRITE STUFF

(Page 56)

Observations
Answers will vary based on results of activity.

LESSON 15: MAKE YOUR OWN INQUIRY!

(Page 57)
All answers will depend on choices students make.

BUILDING TIMELINE SKILLS FOR SOCIAL STUDIES

INTRODUCTION

Timelines give students "the big picture." With a timeline, a student can step back from the individual events and take a global view. Timelines also tell what happened when "just the facts." Because of the visual clarity of their organization, they are more accessible than line after line of text for students who find the general education classroom too challenging.

Skill at designing timelines gives students control over the information they need to understand and apply to their different school assignments. Timelines provide a link to reading instruction because they facilitate understanding both sequence and cause and effect. They synthesize social studies material and enable students to prepare efficiently for assessments. We can also direct students to design a timeline as part of a performance assessment.

By using *Building Timeline Skills for Social Studies,* students acquire useful skills. Timelines are a means for students to learn to synthesize and organize information clearly . Students will use information to design and construct timelines, as well as take information from a timeline and develop it into a structured conversation or a written paragraph.

HOW TO USE THIS BOOK

Three important skills that students need to master are sequencing, synthesizing, and understanding cause/effect relationships. Timelines are efficient ways to help students master these concepts. Students who find pages of text difficult to digest can grasp and utilize information presented in a clear graphic organizer: a timeline.

When students find the general education textbooks extremely challenging, they need a structured, systematic introduction to metacognition. Timelines are part of that introduction. Once students can organize information on a timeline, the social studies text no longer intimidates them. They have learned how to pay attention to headings, dates, italicized and bold print words, captions, and timelines themselves that appear in the textbooks.

In order to use timelines effectively, students need to acquire a variety of skills. This book takes students step by step through the process of synthesizing text into timelines. These are the types of exercises that students will complete in this book:

- Read text and use it to create a timeline.

- Transcribe information from a timeline to a paragraph.

- Construct a timeline from a list of events.

- Design a timeline from a conversation.

- Order events in the proper sequence and place them on a timeline.

- Synthesize information in a timeline that compares and contrasts more than one series of events.

- Gather information and develop a timeline to summarize it.

In particular, students outside the mainstream classrooms need practice in designing timelines. The best way for newcomers to work their way towards using timelines is for their first timelines to be about themselves.

Before starting to work in *Building Timeline Skills for Social Studies,* make several timelines with the class. Here are some suggestions:

- Today's school schedule, by hours

- This week's classroom or school schedule, by days

- The school year so far, by dates

Help students elaborate on each of these by adding personal information. Examples:

- 8:00–missed the bus

- 10:00–went to the counselor

- Tuesday–went home sick

- Thursday–visited my aunt

- September 14–made a goal in soccer

- October 31–took my cousins trick-or-treating

Students need experience working alone, in pairs, in groups, and as a class because that is how they will be expected to function in the workplace. Be sure that students have the opportunity to work in each of these configurations. You might want to start each activity as a class lesson. After students show that they are able to complete the activity, they may work in smaller groups or alone.

Presentation skills are as important in these lessons as they are in every area of the curriculum. Students must learn how to share their work. This sharing takes different formats. Students may show their timeline projects to another student, to a small group, or to the entire class. Students who do not want to participate in this peer-sharing activity may practice sharing alone with the teacher. When they are more skilled at making a presentation, reluctant students can choose a classmate to attend their first peer presentation. Students who still do not want to present to the class may record their presentation and play the recording as they show their work.

Successful assessment outcomes depend on a lot of practice. Give students practice in using the timeline as part of a performance assessment. They will need a clear statement of the criteria with which you will measure their performance. You might choose criteria such as these:

- Organization and care taken in the design and presentation of the timeline, i.e., "How many of your facts are in order?" (1–fewer than five, 3–between six and twelve, 5–more than twelve) "How easy is it to read your timeline?" (1–difficult, 3–easy, 5–very easy).

- Quantity of information presented, i.e., "How many facts did you present?" (1–fewer than five, 3–between six and twelve, 5–more than twelve)

- Accuracy of information presented, i.e., "Is everything correct?" (1–no, 3–almost everything, 5–yes)

- Presentation, i.e. "Did you speak clearly?" (1–no, 3–most of the time, 5–yes) "Did you face the class?" (1–no, 3–most of the time, 5–yes) "Did you ask for questions?" (1–no, 5–yes).

Whether the students have completed the assessment in groups or independently, score their work individually. With a checklist on a clipboard, walk around the classroom as students prepare their timelines. Place a check next to students' names as you observe them doing something you expect, such as searching for evidence to verify information, checking a second source, conferring with a classmate, assisting a team member in designing the timeline, and other skills you expect students to develop.

Practice assessments serve to introduce students to the formal assessment routine that now guides instruction in schools throughout the United States, as state initiatives attempt to strengthen public education.

EXTENSION ACTIVITIES

Have students follow these steps to make a family timeline.

- Students use information about their own families. They make a list for each member, with dates. They find out birth dates and three important events in each family member's life. Then they design a timeline format that they will use for each person. They lay out all the individual timelines, and consolidate them into a single timeline that has information about the entire family on it. Students show their timelines to the class, and select five classmates to ask questions about them.

- In pairs, students cut a 60" piece of yarn. They find one event that happened in each of the last twelve years. Each pair of students needs 12 eight-inch pieces of masking tape. The pieces of tape are wrapped around the yarn every five inches. (This seemingly simple task creates difficulties for students who have had little opportunity to use measuring tools.) Allow enough time for each team to make a neat and well-marked timeline. Be sure that both members of the team work on the measuring task and on the information gathering. Students write one event and its date on each piece of masking tape. Hang these timelines in the classroom, and have each pair of students explain theirs to the class.

- Each student or pair of students selects a state. They locate information about their state in the library or on the Internet. For this activity it is important to select books or Internet sites at a reading level that most of the students can manage. Give students 36 inches of adding machine tape, on which they will make lines at three inch intervals. Students should place dates on the lines at appropriate intervals. If they have twelve years of events, they will number the lines consecutively. If their list of events covers 36 years, each interval will represent 3 years, and so on. This extension activity involves more math than the previous one, and so more time must be allowed for students to lay out the timeline and organize the facts. Under each date, students place the corresponding event. Your students might wish to write the dates and events in color. They can also illustrate their timelines, which can be displayed in the classroom.

- Just as decorators place a designer wallpaper border near the ceiling, you can display a timeline around your classroom walls. Have students design this timeline to reflect the social studies units you study during the year. All dates and events should be very large so students can refer to them from across the room. These timelines can be created on a computer, or by hanging a strip of butcher paper and adding to it as the year, and the study, progress. A sample timeline can include the following:

1920s	1930s	1940s
The Roaring Twenties	Depression	World War II

- Wooden dowels, or even the inside tube from a roll of paper towels or gift wrap, may serve as timelines. Students can put the timeline directly on the dowel or tube, or they can assemble the parts of the timeline on construction paper, cut them out, and attach them to the tube or dowel.

- Turn a broomstick into a timeline. Wrap two sections with tape for hands. Have your students use the rest of the broomstick to create a timeline about a topic you are studying in class. This will be recycled as a study aid when the test or exam on that topic is coming.

- Students put all sorts of artwork on their binders. Have a binder decorating contest, in which binder decorations will be timelines of some period or topic from the social studies curriculum. After students have decorated their binders with an illustrated timeline, display their work. Then have them walk around the room and vote for the two best binder timelines.

- Another way to convert the room into a hall of serious study is for students to transform the legs on tables and desks into timelines. The different events on the timeline can be written on colored paper and taped to the desk or table legs, each leg dedicated to a different period or topic.

- Find a huge spring in a junkyard. Students can create a timeline sculpture out of this spiral by taping events and their dates in chronological order around the spring.

- An effective team project is an audio timeline. Each member of a team of four students has a task:

   Run the recording device.

   Write the script.

   Announce the dates.

   Call out the events.

- A video timeline requires two additional students for the team. One is in charge of gathering illustrations of each event. The other displays these illustrations in front of the camera.

- The slideshow timeline adds technology to the project. If the equipment is available, students prepare a slideshow timeline on the computer.

- A timeline illustrated with photographs is the same as a computer-generated slideshow, but students accomplish it with photos, dates, and captions.

- What timelines can your students create? Alone, in pairs, or on teams, students devise their own timelines. The steps for students to complete in this activity are:

   Decide on a working group.

   Select a topic.

   Choose a way to synthesize information on a timeline.

   Define tasks for everyone in the working group.

   Complete the timeline.

   Decide how to display and present the timeline to the class.

   Assign roles for everyone in the presentation.

   Present the timeline to the class.

ANSWER KEY, BUILDING TIMELINE SKILLS FOR SOCIAL STUDIES

Answers are given where they are definitive. In many instances answers will vary. The integrated feature of the series means students will derive unique answers depending on how they respond to the questions.

LESSON 1: TWENTIETH-CENTURY PRESIDENTS

B. Complete the Timeline (Page 2)

1897–1901	William McKinley
1901–1909	Theodore Roosevelt
1909–1913	William H. Taft
1913–1921	Woodrow Wilson
1921–1923	Warren G. Harding
1923–1929	Calvin Coolidge
1929–1933	Herbert C. Hoover
1933–1945	Franklin D. Roosevelt
1945–1953	Harry S Truman

D. Complete the Paragraph (Page 3)
From 1953 to 1961, Dwight D. Eisenhower was president of the United States. Then it was John F. Kennedy's turn from 1961 to 1963. After that, Lyndon B. Johnson led the country from 1963 to 1969. The next president was Richard M. Nixon, from 1969 to 1974. Gerald R. Ford followed him from 1974 to 1977. In 1977, James (Jimmy) Carter took the job until 1981. After him, Ronald Reagan was president from 1981 to 1989. Who took the job from 1989 to 1993? George Bush did. Next, William (Bill) Clinton became president in 1993. The end of his term: 2001.

E. Make a Timeline (Page 4)
The United States entered World War I in 1917. President: Wilson

World War I ended in 1918. President: Wilson

Women first voted for president in 1920. President: Wilson

The United States entered World War II in 1941. President: Franklin D. Roosevelt

Dr. Martin Luther King, Jr., became a leader in 1955. President: Eisenhower

F. Make a Timeline (Page 5)
The League of Nations was formed in 1920. President: Wilson

The American people got a New Deal in 1933. President : Franklin D. Roosevelt

The United Nations began in 1945. President : Franklin D. Roosevelt

César Chavez organized farm workers in 1962. President: Kennedy

A man landed on the moon in 1969. President: Nixon

The Environmental Protection Agency opened in 1970. President: Nixon

Operation Desert Storm took place in 1991. President: Bush

LESSON 2: THE LABOR MOVEMENT

B. Complete the Sentences (Page 7)
1. The ILGWU was formed in 1900.
2. The Department of Commerce and Labor began in 1903.
3. There was a children's march in Washington DC, in 1903.
4. Massachusetts passed a minimum wage law in 1912.
5. The police in Boston, MA, went on strike in 1919.

C. Make a Timeline (Page 7)

TIMELINE: THE LABOR MOVEMENT (1897–1921)

William McKinley	Theodore Roosevelt	William H. Taft	Woodrow Wilson

1897 1899 1901 1903 1905 1907 1909 1911 1913 1915 1917 1919 1921

ILGWU began.

Department of Commerce and Labor began.
Children's March in Washington D.C.

Massachusetts passed a minimum wage law.

The police in Boston, MA, went on strike.

E. Complete the Paragraphs (Page 8)

In 1929 the <u>Great Depression</u> began. It was a hard time for workers. In <u>1933</u> Frances <u>Perkins</u> became the U.S. secretary of labor. She was the first woman to have this job.

In <u>1934</u> the United States joined the <u>ILO</u> (International Labor Organization). There was a new U.S. law in 1938. It was the <u>Fair Labor Standards Act</u>. It set the minimum wage at 25 cents an hour. Some people worked more than 40 hours a week. The extra time was <u>overtime</u>. People got more money for each hour of overtime.

In <u>1941</u> the United States entered <u>World War II</u>. This war ended in <u>1945</u>. In <u>1949</u>, the <u>Fair Labor Standards Act</u> changed. There were more laws against <u>child labor</u>.

G. Match These (Page 9)

1. c. gives older workers the same rights as younger workers
2. d. says that jobs must be open to all people
3. a. says that men and women must get the same pay for the same work
4. b. was the minimum wage in 1978

H. Make a Timeline (Page 9)

1963: Congress passed a new law. It was called the Equal Pay Act.
1964: Congress passed another law. it was called the Civil Rights Act.
1967: Congress passed the Age Discrimination in Employment Act.
1978: The U.S. minimum wage was $2.65 per hour.

LESSON 3: WORLD ORGANIZATIONS

B. Make a Timeline (Page 10)

In 1918, World War I ended.
In 1920, the League of Nations started.
In 1933, Germany and Japan left the League of Nations.
In 1934, the Soviet Union joined.
In 1939, World War II began.
In 1946, the League of Nations ended.

D. Match These (Page 11)

1. e. The UN began.
2. b. Seventeen more countries joined the UN.
3. c. UN workers won the Nobel Peace Prize
4. a. The UN had a meeting about children.
5. d. The Earth Summit was held in Brazil.

E. Make a Timeline (Page 12)

1945: The UN began. President: Franklin D. Roosevelt
1960: Seventeen more countries joined the UN. President: Eisenhower
1988: UN workers won the Nobel Peace Prize. President: Reagan
1990: The UN had a meeting about children. President: Bush
1992: The Earth Summit was held in Brazil. President: Bush

F. Complete the Timeline (Page 13)

1913: Woodrow Wilson became president.
1918: World War I ended
1920: The League of Nations started.
1933: Franklin D. Roosevelt became president.
1939: World War II began
1945: The United Nations started.
1946: The League of Nations ended.
1981: Ronald Reagan became president
1988: UN workers won the Nobel Peace prize.

G. Complete the Paragraphs (Page 13)

Woodrow Wilson became president in 1913. During his term, <u>World War I</u> ended in 1918. The <u>League of Nations</u> began in 1920.

The League of Nations could not keep peace in the world. <u>World War II</u> began in 1939. <u>Franklin D. Roosevelt</u> was president of the United States. The <u>United Nations</u> began in 1945. It replaced the <u>League of Nations</u>, which ended in <u>1946</u>. In <u>1988</u>, UN workers won the <u>Nobel Peace Prize</u>. <u>Ronald Reagan</u> was president of the United States at the time.

LESSON 4: THE 19TH AMENDMENT

B. Complete the Timeline (Page 14)

1890	Wyoming
1900	Colorado
1900	Idaho
1900	Utah
1914	Montana
1914	Nevada

C. Match These (Page 15)

1. f. Some women met in New York.
2. g. Women could vote in Wyoming.
3. b. Women could vote in Colorado, Idaho, and Utah.
4. e. Women could vote in Montana and Nevada.
5. a. The first woman was elected to Congress.
6. c. The 19th Amendment was approved.
7. d. Women first voted for president.

D. Make a Timeline (Page 15)

1848: Some women met in New York.
1890: Women could vote in Wyoming.
1900: Women could vote in Colorado, Idaho, and Utah.
1914: Women could vote in Montana and Nevada.
1916: The first woman was elected to Congress.
1919: The 19th Amendment was approved.
1920: Women first voted for president.

F. Circle the Answer (Page 16)

west

LESSON 5: THE NEW DEAL

B. Complete the Sentences (Page 18)

1. FDR made a plan in <u>1933</u>.
2. About ten million people were out of work in <u>1939</u>.
3. FDR became president in <u>1933</u>.
4. The WPA began in <u>1935</u>.

D. Match These (Page 19)

1. c. NYA
2. d. FSA
3. b. FCC
4. e. FCIC
5. a. CCC

E. Complete the Paragraph (Page 19)

There were many New Deal agencies. In <u>1933</u> the Civilian Conservation Corps (CCC) opened. It helped people get jobs. In <u>1934</u> the <u>Federal Communication Commission</u> (FCC) opened. It made rules about <u>radios and telephones</u>. The <u>National Youth Administration</u> opened in 1935. It helped <u>students</u> get jobs. In <u>1937</u> the <u>Farm Security Administration</u> (FSA) opened. It helped <u>farmers</u> get <u>machinery</u>. In 1938 an agency opened to help <u>farmers who lost crops</u>. It was the <u>Federal Crop Insurance Corporation</u> (FCIC).

F. Make a Timeline (Page 20)

TIMELINE: THE NEW DEAL IN HISTORY

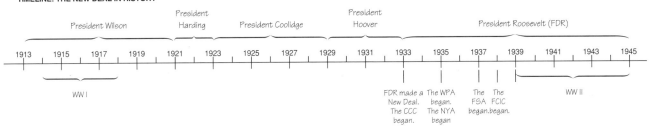

LESSON 6: GENERATIONS

B. Answer the Questions (Page 22)
1. October 29, 1929
2. 1927
3. 1927
4. 1927
5. 1921
6. 1926
7. 1920
8. 1929

C. Make a Timeline (Page 23)
1920: Automakers sold about 1.9 million cars.
1921: *Three Soldiers* was published.
1926: *The Sun Also Rises* was published.
1927: Charles Lindbergh flew across the Atlantic.
Elmer Gantry was published.
People watched the first important talkie.
1929: Automakers sold almost 4.5 million cars.
The Great Depression started.

E. Match These (Page 24)
1. f. World War II ended.
2. d. The baby boomers were born.
3. a. Many Americans bought televisions.
4. g. Baby boomers wanted peace.
5. c. Health and fitness were important.
6. e. Baby boomers worried about the world.
7. b. Baby boomers led the country.

F. Make a Timeline (Page 25)
1950s: Baby boomers moved to suburbs, bought televisions.
1960s: Baby boomers wanted change and peace.
1970s: Fitness and health were important. Baby boomers got jobs and started families.
1980s: Baby boomers worried about the world. They wanted a good life for their children.
1990s: Baby boomers ran the country. They were in charge of hospitals, schools, industry. Bill Clinton became the first baby boomer president.

LESSON 7: A HEALTHY NATION

B. Find the Details (Page 26)
Dates: 1796, 1885, 1896, 1952.
Men's names: Dr. Edward Jenner, Dr. Louis Pasteur, Wilhelm Kolle, Dr. Jonas Salk.
Names of sicknesses: smallpox, rabies, typhoid, cholera, polio.

C. Match These (Page 26)
1. d. smallpox 1796
2. c. rabies 1885
3. a. cholera 1896
4. e. typhoid 1896
5. b. polio 1952

D. Make a Timeline (Page 27)
1796: Dr. Edward Jenner made the smallpox vaccine.
1885: Dr. Louis Pasteur made a vaccine for rabies.
1896: Wilhelm Kolle made vaccines for cholera and typhoid.
1952: Jonas Salk made the polio vaccine.

F. Circle the Answer (Page 28)
1. 1992
2. 1994
3. 1970
4. 1994

G. Complete the Timeline (Page 29)
1970: The EPA began.
1970: Americans recycled 7% of their trash.
1974: 15 million gallons of oil spilled into U.S. waters every year.
1990: bad air in 199 cities
1992: two million gallons of oil spilled
1994: bad air in 70 cities
1994: Americans recycled 24% of their trash.

LESSON 8: BASEBALL AND BASKETBALL

B. Complete the Sentences (Page 30)
1. <u>Satchel Paige</u> was a great pitcher. He joined the <u>Cleveland Indians</u> in 1948.
2. In 1947 <u>Jackie Robinson</u> joined the <u>Brooklyn Dodgers</u>.
3. <u>Babe Ruth</u> was a great home-run hitter. In the 1920s, he played for the <u>New York Yankees</u>.

C. Circle the Answer (Page 31)
1. New York
2. the Cincinnati Red Stockings
3. the National League
4. Jackie Robinson

D. Make a Timeline (Page 31)
1845: first baseball club
1869: Cincinnati Red Stockings
1876: National League
1900: American League
1920s: Babe Ruth
1947: Jackie Robinson
1948: Satchel Paige

F. Match These (Page 32)
1. d. James Naismith invented basketball.
2. f. Metal hoops were first used.
3. c. Backboards were added to hoops.
4. h. The first professional league began.
5. b. Baskets with holes were first used.
6. a. The NBA began.
7. e. Women's basketball became an Olympic event.
8. g. The first WNBA games were played.

G. Make a Timeline (Page 33)
1891 Naismith invented basketball.
1893 Metal hoops
1894 Backboards were added
1896 The first professional league began.
1913 Baskets with holes were first used.
1949 The NBA began.
1976 Women's basketball became an Olympic event.
1997 The first WNBA games were played.

LESSON 9: TENNIS, GOLF, AND SKIING

B. Complete the Timeline (Page 34)
1000 years ago: Tennis started in France.
1874: Outerbridge brought tennis to U.S.
1881: an association formed
1927: Gibson was born.
1943: King and Ashe were born.
1952: Connors was born.

D. Find the Details (Page 35)
1. 1894
2. 1916
3. 1948
4. 1980

E. Make a Timeline (Page 35)
1894: USGA
1916: PGA
1948: LPGA
1980: Senior PGA

G. Make a Timeline (Page 36)
1930s: Americans wanted to ski
1948: Gretchen Fraser won a gold medal
1960s: About 400 ski areas opened in the United States

H. Make a Timeline (Page 37)
1874: tennis came to U.S.
1881: USTA began
1894: USGA began
1916: PGA began
1927: Gibson born
1948: Fraser won Olympic medal
1952: Connors born

LESSON 10: SPACE EXPLORATION

B. Match These (Page 38)
1. b. a U.S. rocket traveled 250 miles into space.
2. c. The USSR launched *Sputnik I*.
3. a. NASA began.
4. d. The first U.S. satellite was launched.

C. Make a Timeline (Page 38)
1949: A U.S. rocket traveled 250 miles into space.
1957: The USSR launched Sputnik I.
1958: NASA began.
1958: The first U.S. satellite was launched.

E. Complete the Timeline (Page 39)
1958: NASA opens
1961: First American goes into space
1969: First people land on the moon
1973: Manned lab begins to orbit earth
1981: Manned space shuttle goes up.

G. Answer the Questions (Page 40)
1. July 1969
2. March 1969
3. April 1970
4. December 1968
5. December 1972

I. Make a Timeline (Page 41)

Enterprise 1977
Columbia 1981
Challenger 1983

LESSON 11: MILITARY CONFLICTS

B. Complete the Timeline (Page 42)

March 1960: Eisenhower says yes to a plan.
January 1961: Kennedy becomes president.
April 17, 1961: Exiles invade the Bay of Pigs.
April 19, 1961: The fighting stops.

D. Make a Timeline (Page 43)

October 16, 1962: photos of weapon sites
October 22, 1962: Kennedy on TV
October 24, 1962: first letter from Khrushchev to Kennedy
October 26, 1962: second letter
October 27, 1962: third letter
October 28, 1962: Khrushchev agrees to take arms out of Cuba

G. Complete the Timeline (Page 45)

August 2, 1990: Iraq invaded Kuwait.
August 7, 1990: U.S. troops went to Saudi Arabia.
January 15, 1991: The UN set a deadline.
January 17, 1991: Operation Desert Storm began.
February 26, 1991: Hussein told Iraqi troops to leave Kuwait.
February 28, 1991: U.S. and other troops stopped fighting.
April 11, 1991: UN ended the war.

LESSON 12: ARIZONA, CALIFORNIA, AND FLORIDA

B. Answer the Questions (Page 46)

1. 1912
2. 1948
3. 1960s and 1970s
4. 1970s
5. 1985
6. 1990

D. Complete the Paragraphs (Page 47)

Between 1910 and 1915, Hollywood became the movie center of the world. In the 1930s, many poor farmers went to California. Many people had no jobs. During World War II, Californians made planes, ships, and weapons.

In the 1960s, water was a problem. In the 1970s, people in California worried about clean air and clean water.

During the 1980s, the population grew more than 25 percent. By the 1990s, 44 cities had more than one hundred thousand people.

In 1991 California had more than 22 million vehicles!

F. Find the Details (Page 48)

Dates: 1920s
1929
1945
1960s
1980s
1980
1990

G. Complete the Timeline (Page 49)

1920s: land boom
1929: land prices dropped
1945: became popular vacation place
1945: many older people moved there
1960s: Cuban people moved there
1980s: Cuban people moved there
1980–1990: population increased more than 32 percent

LESSON 13: ILLINOIS AND TEXAS

A. Make a Timeline (Page 50)

1900: Illinois was number three among states in manufacturing.
1920s: A system of highways was built.
1930s: Manufacturing dropped during the Great Depression.
1937: Southeast Illinois had an oil boom.
1939–1945: More jobs and money went to Illinois during World War II.
1980–1990: The state population did not grow much.

C. Complete the Timeline (Page 51)

1901: A big oil well erupted.
after 1901: Much oil was found.
1920s and 1930s: Big highways were built.
after WWII: Manufacturing grew.
1940–1980: The population doubled.
1980s: Oil prices fell.
1980–1990: The population grew more than 19 percent.

D. Match These (Page 52)

1. d. AZ
2. c. CA
3. a. FL
4. e. IL
5. b. TX

E. Make a Timeline (Page 52 - 53)

TIMELINE: FIVE STATES

	1900	1910	1920	1930	1940	1950	1960	1970	1980	1990
AZ		Became a state in 1912				Native Americans could vote	Many factories opened	Population grew more than 50%	CAP moved water to Phoenix	CAP moved water to Tucson
CA			Hollywood becomes movie center of world	Many poor farmers went to California	Californians made planes, ships, weapons		Water was a problem	People worried about clean air and water	Population grew more than 25%; CA had the most cars	44 cities had more than 100,000 people
FL			Land boom		Land prices drop	Florida becomes a popular vacation place	Cubans come	Cubans come	The population grew 35%	
IL	#3 among states in manufacturing		A system of highways was built	Manufacturing dropped during Great Depression	Southeast IL had oil boom	Jobs and money went to IL			State population didn't grow much	
TX	1st oil well erupted	People found more oil	Big highways built		Population doubled 1940–1980	Manufacturing grew			Oil prices dropped	

LESSON 14: SOME IMPORTANT AMERICANS

B. Make a Timeline (Page 54)
1907: was born
1929: graduated from college
1932: received master's degree
1941: *Under the Sea Wind* published
1951: *The Sea Around Us* published
1955: *The Edge of the Sea* published
1962: *Silent Spring* published

D. Complete the Paragraphs (Page 55)
Maria Tallchief was born in <u>1925</u>. She was born on the Osage Indian reservation in Oklahoma. She danced. She became famous all over the world. She was the first American ballerina that everyone knew.

Tallchief danced in Monte Carlo from <u>1942</u> to <u>1947</u>. She danced in New York from <u>1947</u> to <u>1965</u>. In <u>1958</u> she became a mother. She stopped dancing in <u>1965</u>. This surprised people. They wanted her to dance more.

Tallchief went to Chicago. There she taught ballet. She started the Chicago City Ballet. Tallchief was the director of the Chicago City Ballet from <u>1980</u> to <u>1987</u>.

F. Complete the Timeline (Page 56)
1927: Chavez born in Arizona.
1944: Chavez joined the U.S. Navy.
1962: He started the National Farm Workers Association.
1993: Chavez died.
1994: President Clinton honored him.

H. Answer the Questions (Page 57)
1. 1929
2. 1948
3. 1953
4. 1955
5. 1963
6. 1964

I. Complete the Timeline (Page 57)
Born: 1929
Graduated: 1948
Married: 1953
Worked for Rights: 1955
"I have a dream": 1963
Nobel Peace Prize: 1964

LESSON 15: YOUR OWN TIMELINES
Answers will vary for all sections, depending on students' information.

BUILDING WRITING SKILLS FOR SOCIAL STUDIES

INTRODUCTION

Building Writing Skills for Social Studies has 15 lessons. The first five concentrate on sentence formation. The second five continue to teach the formation of sentences and introduce paragraph development. The third section works more on paragraph development, while continuing to teach and review sentences.

Responses are not left to chance or students' intuition. Why?

- We want our reluctant writers to be successful.

- An error made in writing is an error reinforced.

- Non-native speakers will be able to teach the material with confidence.

- Fluency, generating a lot of written language, is the first step. The first step toward fluency is pencil to paper.

- More of our new students each year come to us underserved by previous schooling; we must get ready for them.

- Many of the exercises can be done independently.

HOW TO USE THIS BOOK

The lessons are arranged in chronological order, and the level of difficulty increases as learners progress through the book.

Prior to starting their work in this book, students need pencil-to-paper practice. When given a writing assignment, many reluctant writers have not written a single word by the end of the period. Most of them do not believe that they can write. Spend several brief sessions on the following exercise as you prepare to start the work on this book.

Part A:

1. Give students an easy topic such as "This School," "The Weather," "My Friend," or "Soccer."

2. Make a semantic web of the topic on the board.

    Example:

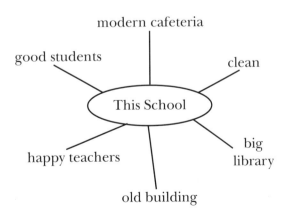

3. Ask students to be silent for one minute as they think about the topic and study the web.

4. Say "Write," and give students three minutes to write about the topic.

5. Say "Stop," and have students count how many words they wrote.

6. Provide graph paper for them to graph their daily results.

7. Celebrate large jumps in the number of words, even if students must copy from the group-generated web initially in order to write something down.

8. Post progress graphs on a wall to illustrate success.

When most students are writing every day, move to Part B. This part of the preparation is exactly the same as Part A, with the omission of the semantic web. If students get this practice daily at the same time, and with the same procedure, most will be ready to move from Part A to Part B after one week, and ready to start working in the book after two weeks.

A word about technical accuracy . . . Yes, we expect our students to produce excellent work that is mechanically correct. That is part of a well-designed outcome. Some of the students who can benefit from this book might not be close to producing the desired outcome yet, however. For them, it is important to encourage a lot of writing before insisting on correct writing. The greater risk-taking behavior we can promote in beginning writers, the greater volume of writing they will produce. Instead of resting their heads on their desks in despair when given an assignment, they will dig in and try to write more words than they did before.

If we do not pay attention to mechanics at the beginning, when is the right time to expect technically excellent work? As students develop confidence in producing a lot of writing, we can tell them that soon their writing will be good enough to correct. And when it is good enough to correct, it will be good enough to post on the walls of the classroom. After the first couple of students work to revise and produce technically excellent writing, other, competitive students will strive to be among those whose work is displayed.

Undoubtedly, there will still be reluctant writers who neither take risks nor push themselves to write more. It is important to display their work, too. However, work must be correct before it is displayed. Some students need us to rewrite their first passages for them to copy. Use an easy-to-read font and a large print size. Skip lines. Then assign the student to copy the rewrite. The goal for the class must be that everyone submits his or her work to revision so that all work may be celebrated and displayed.

Lesson 1

This is a warm-up lesson. It introduces the presidents. As they complete this lesson, learners will write a lot and gain confidence in their ability to handle the material. First, they study a table and complete a list to locate and transcribe information. This is the information they will use throughout the lesson.

In Activity B, page 3, students copy sentences to practice sentence form. The exercises in C, page 3, assist learners in referencing lists and composing statements. In D, page 3, they again practice sentence form by copying sentences. Activity E, page 4, contains sentence writing exercises like those in activity B. Activity F, page 4, provides practice in writing the native speaker short response. Together with Activity G, page 4, it reinforces this natural way to answer questions orally. Activity H, page 5, Activity I, page 5, and Activity J, page 6, introduce writing when- questions. The final activity, Activity K, page 6, introduces who-questions and reinforces the short response.

When students have completed Lesson 1, they know that they are capable of doing the activities in the book and will already have done some writing.

Lessons 2 to 5

These lessons begin with a reading passage that students copy in Activity A, *Copy the passage*, for writing practice. In Activity B, *Find these words in the passage*, they scan the passage to locate words and prepare a slot-filler activity. Next, they refer to the passage and supply missing words for an incomplete version of it. This is Activity C, *Write the missing words in the blanks,* and it reinforces students' understanding of how words fit into sentences and sentences into passages.

Activity D, *Write the word or words from the passage that have the same meaning,* is a paraphrasing activity in which learners refer again to the passage to find words with the same meaning as other words in a list. Activity E, *Work with the "starts" and "ends" of sentences,* again requires learners to refer to the passage and form statements from two halves. They then write the complete statement to practice the simple sentence form. Activity F, *Answer these questions,* is a cued writing activity in which learners respond to wh- questions (who, what, where, when, why).

Lesson 6

Activity A, *Underline these sentences in the passage,* page 23, is a skimming activity that provides practice in a study skill. Students will need to highlight important parts of passages as they move into more complicated and challenging text. In Activity B, *Find the sentence in A that means the same as each of these,* page 24, learners practice paraphrasing as they work on vocabulary development and comprehension.

Activity C, *Answer these questions about the passage,* page 24, introduces cause and effect, constructing statements with because, and developing responses from the question. Students often do not realize how easy it is to use the words that form a question to construct the response.

In Activity D, *Put numbers next to these sentences to show the correct order,* students practice sequencing, and they get an introduction to paragraph development. After they complete Lesson 6, students will have a basis for beginning to construct paragraphs.

Lessons 7 to 10

These lessons follow the same format as Lesson 6. However, an additional activity at the end of each lesson guides students as they respond to a topic-specific question. Activity E is a list of facts about the topic. Students insert the facts in a formula paragraph that resembles beginning sequential writing. This introduces writing statements in sequential order and using connectors to make smooth transitions.

Lessons 11 to 15

Activity A, *Highlight or circle these words and dates in the passage,* provides more practice in skills students will need to take notes. In Activity B, *Now put what you highlighted into this outline,* students follow cues to prepare a topic outline. Activity C, *Read the answers,* drills the form of wh- questions. Activity D is the same as Activity E in Lessons 7 through 10, however students use different connectors in this paragraph. In Activity E, *The sentences below have the same information* students read paraphrases of sentences in the original passage. These paraphrases are out of sequence, however. Students will put them in order and write out the new paragraph. This reviews sequencing and paraphrasing.

By the end of this book students will have acquired several strategies for using writing as a study tool and as a way to improve their understanding of text. They will be ready to try to write their own paragraphs in response to social studies material. Most important, they will know that they can write clear, sequential passages.

EXTENSION ACTIVITIES

• To review a unit, or as part of a performance assessment, students write a statement, or even a paragraph, about one aspect of a current social studies lesson. Collect the statements and distribute them to other students who will place them under the correct heading on a bulletin board. Possible headings for the topic "the 1990s": Jobs, NAFTA, Technology.

Possible statements for the topic "the 1990s":

1993—7 of 100 out of work

1997—5 of 100 out of work

North American Free Trade Agreement

Canada, Mexico, and the U.S.

Use of computers and connections

- To give background practice for the eventual compare-and-contrast assignment, assign students to teams of two or four, and ask them to make and complete a graphic organizer with statements of similarities and differences about a topic.

TOPIC: —————————— and ——————————

How are they the same? How are they different?

- To prepare students for the descriptive mode of writing, place a large illustration in front of the class. Some examples: a city surrounded by smog; a room full of technology. As students suggest words and phrases to describe each illustration, write their suggestions on the board. Then students do a timed writing in which they try to write as many statements as possible to describe the illustration.

- Invite competent writers in the class, parent volunteers, instructional assistants, and peer tutors to help correct and improve the paragraphs. Then students can share them in a "four corners" activity. For this activity, students number off from one to four. All those students numbered "one" go to one corner of the room, those numbered "two" to another, etc. In these new groups, they read aloud what they have written.

- In small groups, students prepare Venn diagrams for display in the classroom. These diagrams synthesize information and make it easier to understand. They also serve to prepare writers for compare-and-contrast writing. Select two topics, events, or periods, each of which goes on one side of the diagram. When students find a similarity, it goes in the middle, where the ovals overlap.

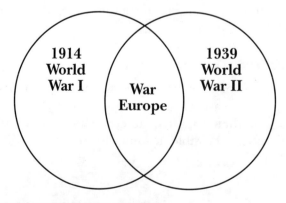

- To give students experience using writing as a tool of communication, set up a pen pal exchange. The pen pals can be halfway around the world, or in the same class. The medium can be E-mail or handwritten messages placed in classroom mailboxes.

- To maximize learning, suggest curriculum-related topics. If we tell students to write about the social studies unit, they often find it boring. However, if we suggest they play a written "jeopardy" game, in which they supply the answers and the pen pal has to search for the questions, they find it more exciting. They can make crossword puzzles and word searches for their pen pals. Sometimes the pen pal exchange is across the miles, and both schools have the same software and operating systems. If this is the case, your students can use this activity to improve their technology skills by attaching these puzzles to E-mail correspondence.

- Students copy one of the passages from the book, substituting lines for every fifth, eighth, or tenth word. They exchange papers and fill in the missing words on their classmates' passages. This serves as a review of the lesson topic, as it gives students practice at looking for details in a paragraph. In this case, the details are in the missing words.

- To enhance students' vocabulary and give them writing practice, select a passage from the mainstream text. Rewrite it by paraphrasing each sentence in more accessible language. Then scramble the rewritten sentences. Students will refer to the original as they work in pairs or small groups to order the rewrite. Then each student makes a copy of the new passage.

- To stimulate writing fluency, have each student write a question about the lesson topic. This question should be placed at the top of a piece of notebook paper. Students sit in groups of six or eight. At a signal, they pass their questions to the right. Taking the paper from the student on their left, they read the question and attempt to answer it. After two minutes, at another signal, they again pass their papers to the person on their right. This continues until each student has his or her original paper.

- To give students practice with word processing, have students take the paragraphs they have written that has been revised. The students then highlight key words and phrases. At the computer, they use a different color (if a color printer is available) or italics or bold print to make these words and phrases stand out. This assignment can serve as a review for a test. It can also be part of a performance assessment.

ANSWER KEY, BUILDING WRITING SKILLS FOR SOCIAL STUDIES

Answers are given where they are definitive. In many instances answers will vary. The integrated feature of the series means students will derive unique answers depending on how they respond to the questions.

LESSON 1: THE PRESIDENCY

A. (Page 2)
1, 1st; 2, 2nd; 3, 3rd; 4, 4th; 5, 5th; 6, 6th; 7, 7th; 8, 8th; 9, 9th; 10, 10th; 11, 11th; 12, 12th; 13, 13th; 14, 14th; 15, 15th; 16, 16th; 17, 17th; 18, 18th; 19, 19th; 20, 20th; 21, 21st; 22, 22nd, 23, 23rd; 24, 24th; 25, 25th; 26, 26th; 27, 27th; 28, 28th; 29, 29th; 30, 30th; 31, 31st; 32, 32nd; 33, 33rd; 34, 34th; 35, 35th; 36, 36th; 37, 37th; 38, 38th; 39, 39th; 40, 40th; 41, 41st; 42, 42nd.

B. (Page 3)
George Washington was the first president.
James Buchanan was the fifteenth president.
Warren G. Harding was the twenty-ninth president.

C. (Page 3)
Abraham Lincoln was the 16th president.
    (For questions 2–5, students' answers will vary. Check to make sure they use ordinal numbers in their sentences.)

D. (Page 3)
1. Andrew Johnson was president from 1865 to 1869.
2. Dwight D. Eisenhower was president from 1953 to 1961.
3. Gerald R. Ford was president from 1974 to 1977.

E. (Page 4)
Sample: James K. Polk was president from 1845 to 1849.
    (Students' sentences will vary.)

F. (Page 4)
1. From 1869 to 1877.
2. From 1913 to 1921.
3. From 1897 to 1901.

G. (Page 4)
1. From 1801 to 1809.
2. In 1881.
3. From 1901 to 1909.
4. From 1961 to 1963.

H. (Page 5)
1. When was James Madison president?
2. When was Rutherford B. Hayes president?
3. When was Jimmy Carter president?

I. (Page 5)
When was George Bush president?
When was James Madison president?
When was James Buchanan president?
When was Chester A. Arthur president?
When was Grover Cleveland president?

J. (Page 6)
Sample: When was Andrew Johnson president?
From 1865 to 1869.
    (Students' sentences will vary.)

K. (Page 6)
Who was president from 1909 to 1913?
Who was president from 1923 to 1929?
Who was president from 1929 to 1933?

LESSON 2: 1900 TO 1910

A. (Page 7)
Students copy the complete passage on page 7 of the student text.

B. (Page 8)
Students should circle a total of 17 words or phrases in the passage on page 7.

C. (Page 8)
    President McKinley <u>served</u> from 1897 to 1901. In 1898, Cuba and Spain were <u>at war.</u>
    The United States <u>sent</u> a ship to Cuba. The name of the ship was <u>Maine.</u> Spain <u>did not</u> like this. Spain <u>thought</u> the United States <u>wanted to help</u> Cuba. The <u>Maine exploded.</u> Then the Americans were mad. They <u>went to war</u> against Spain. This was the <u>Spanish-American War of 1898.</u>
    <u>After</u> the war, the United States <u>got</u> more land from Spain. It now <u>had</u> Puerto Rico, Guam, and the Philippines.
    McKinley also made Hawaii a <u>U.S. territory.</u> Hawaii <u>became</u> a state in 1959.

President Theodore Roosevelt <u>served</u> from 1901 to 1909. He <u>loved</u> nature. He made more <u>national parks.</u> He also <u>worked to create</u> the Panama Canal.

D. (Page 9)
1. served
2. war
3. wanted to help
4. exploded
5. loved

E. (Page 9)
1. When McKinley was president, Cuba and Spain were at war.
2. When McKinley was president, the Maine exploded.
3. When McKinley was president, there was a war.
4. When Roosevelt was president, more land became national parks.
5. When Roosevelt was president, people worked on the Panama Canal.

F. (Page 10)
1. He was president from 1897 to 1901.
2. He made Hawaii a territory.
3. He was president from 1901 to 1909.
4. He loved nature.
5. He worked to create the Panama Canal.

LESSON 3: 1910 TO 1920

A. (Page 11)
Students copy the entire passage on page 11 of the student text.

B. (Page 12)
Students circle 16 words or phrases in the passage on page 11.

C. (Page 12)
Students should copy the following words or phrases in the blanks:

Almost six million people <u>immigrated</u> to the United States between 1911 and 1920. That was not <u>as many as</u> had come between 1901 and 1910. Almost 9 million people had come during those years.

William H. Taft was president from 1909 to 1913. He always <u>wanted to be a judge.</u> When he was president, work hours changed. <u>People who worked</u> for the government worked <u>eight hours a day.</u> The U.S. Department of Labor opened in 1913. It helps workers. After Taft was president, he was a judge.

Woodrow Wilson was president from 1913 to 1921. He <u>wanted to work on</u> problems <u>at home.</u> When he was president, there was a law against child labor.

In 1914, the Panama Canal opened. In 1914, there was also a <u>war in Europe.</u> It was a big war. Wilson <u>did not want to go to war.</u> On April 6, 1917, the United States <u>went to war.</u> It fought on the same side as Belgium, Britain, France, Greece, Japan, Montenegro, Romania, Russia, Serbia and many other countries.

Men from the United States <u>went to fight.</u> Women <u>worked in factories.</u> They <u>did the work</u> men <u>had done.</u> This was World War I. It ended in 1918.

D. (Page 13)
1. immigrated
2. as many as
3. People who worked for
4. eight hours a day
5. opened
6. wanted to work on
7. went to fight
8. went to war
9. worked in factories
10. did the work

E. (Page 13)
1. Nearly six million people immigrated to the U.S. from 1910 to 1920.
2. Taft had always wished to be a judge.
3. The Department of Labor began in 1913.
4. After Taft left the presidency, he became a judge.
5. Wilson wanted to stay out of war.
6. Wilson hoped to solve problems at home.
7. Women went to work in factories.

F. (Page 14)
1. William H. Taft was president from 1909 to 1913.
2. It opened in 1913.
3. Woodrow Wilson was president from 1913 to 1921.
4. The Panama Canal opened in 1914.

LESSON 4: WORLD WAR I

A. (Page 15)
Students should copy the entire passage on page 15 of the student text.

B. (Page 16)
Students should circle 15 words or phrases in the passage.

C. (Page 16)
World War I was "the war to end all wars." It began in 1914. It started in Europe. Many countries fought in this war.

The countries in the war had _armies._ Armies are groups of people who fight. They fight to protect their country. Armies need _arms_ to fight. Arms are guns and other weapons. The countries in the war built war plants. War plants were big factories. These factories made arms.

After the war, there were new countries. Austria-Hungary became Austria, Hungary, and Czechoslovakia. After the war, the Republic of Turkey was formed.

Life for women changed. During the war, women had worked in offices. They had worked in factories, too. When the war ended, women in the United States wanted to keep their jobs. After the war, women in the United States got the vote. They could vote for president for the first time.

D. (Page 17)
1. "the war to end all wars"
2. began
3. Many countries
4. fought
5. armies
6. to protect their country
7. war plants
8. arms
9. After the war
10. was formed
11. factories
12. to keep their jobs

E. (Page 17)
1. World War I was called "the war to end all wars."
2. World War I started in 1914.
3. War plants make arms.
4. People in an army fight in a war.
5. The Republic of Turkey was formed after the war.
6. Women wanted to keep their new jobs.

F. (Page 18)
1. World War I was "the war to end all wars."
2. World War I began in 1914.
3. After the war, there were new countries.
4. Austria-Hungary became Austria, Hungary, and Czechoslovakia.
5. The Republic of Turkey was formed.
6. Women had worked in factories during the war.
7. Women wanted to keep their jobs.
8. Women got the vote.

LESSON 5: THE 1920S

A. (Page 19)
Students should copy the entire passage on page 19 of the student text.

B. (Page 20)
Students should circle 14 words and phrases in the passage on page 19.

C. (Page 20)
Warren G. Harding was president from 1921 to 1923. In 1921 and 1924, the United States cut back on immigration. This means it limited immigration. Fewer people could move to the United States.

Calvin Coolidge was president from 1923 to 1929. He said, "The business of America is business." He wanted the country's businesses to grow. They did. The United States was rich. Many people had good jobs in factories and offices. Artists, writers, and musicians had work. People could get credit. They could buy now and pay later. Many people now worked 5 1/2 days a week. So they had more time to relax. By the 1920s, people could go to the movies. They had radios.

By 1927, many families had cars. People needed good roads. They needed gas for their cars. Gas stations were built. They needed to eat on the road. _Diners_ were built. These are small restaurants. People needed a place to sleep. Cabins were built near roads. Today we call them motels.

By 1929, companies had made many products. They could not sell all of them. They lost money. People lost jobs. The good times ended. The Great Depression began.

D. (Page 21)
1. cut back on
2. could move to
3. musicians
4. fewer people
5. credit

E. (Page 21)

1. Warren G. Harding was president from 1921 to 1923.
2. Calvin Coolidge was president from 1923 to 1929.
3. The business of America is business.
4. The United States was rich.
5. Many families had cars.
6. People needed gasoline for their cars.
7. In 1929, people were out of work
8. The good times were over.

F. (Page 22)

1. Warren G. Harding was president from 1921 to 1923.
2. The United States cut back on immigration.
3. He was president from 1923 to 1929.
4. He said, "The business of America is business."
5. They could get credit.
6. They needed to eat on the road.
7. They had made many products.
8. People lost jobs.

LESSON 6: THE 1930S

A. (Page 23)

Students find and underline each sentence.

B. (Page 24)

1. Strong business means more jobs.
2. Thirteen million had no jobs.
3. In 1939, ten million people still had no work.
4. The only thing we have to fear is fear itself.
5. There were few jobs.
6. Public works jobs put people to work.

C. (Page 24)

1. Life was hard for many Americans because there were few jobs.
2. The government gave money to businesses because it wanted to help them.
3. They listened to their radios because FDR talked to them.
4. FDR said "The only thing we have to fear is fear itself" because he did not want people to be afraid.
5. She went all over the country because she wanted to help FDR in his work.

D. (Page 25)

In the first part of Exercise D, the order of the numbers is 6, 4, 3, 5, 1, 2.

The correct order of the sentences is

1. Herbert Hoover was president from 1929 to 1933.
2. In 1933, thirteen million people were out of work.
3. Hoover's government gave money to businesses.
4. Franklin D. Roosevelt was president from 1933 to 1945.
5. He talked to people on the radio.
6. Ten million people were out of work in 1939.

LESSON 7: WORLD WAR II

A. (Page 26)

Students find and underline each sentence.

B. (Page 27)

1. Many people were homeless.
2. All wanted peace.
3. A big war industry began.
4. Women worked in industry.
5. Many people could find work now.

C. (Page 27)

1. Women got jobs because men went to war.
2. Factories made planes because planes flew in this war.
3. Factories were ruined because bombs fell on cities.
4. Many people were homeless because their homes were ruined in the war.
5. They met to form the United Nations because all wanted peace.

D. (Page 28)

In the first part of Exercise D, the correct order of the numbers is 3, 5, 1, 4, 2.

The correct order of the sentences is

1. World War II began.
2. The United States entered the war.
3. The United States, China, Great Britain, and the Soviet Union met in Moscow.
4. The United Nations planners met in Washington, D.C.
5. They opened the United Nations at a meeting in San Francisco.

E. (Page 28)

The blanks in the paragraph should be filled in as follows:

(1) men went to war
(2) women went to work in war plants
(3) people in other countries lost their homes
(4) everyone wanted peace

LESSON 8: THE 1940S

A. (Page 29)

Students find and underline each sentence.

B. (Page 30)

1. People bought cars in large numbers right after the war.
2. He took responsibility for government actions.
3. The buck stops here.
4. They said to attack one was to attack all.
5. People used automatic washing machines for the first time.
6. He also wanted people in other countries to be free.

C. (Page 30)

1. Truman said, "The buck stops here" because he took responsibility.
2. Truman made the Truman Doctrine because he wanted all people to be free.
3. It is called the baby boom because many babies were born.
4. Auto plants were making cars again because the war was over.
5. People could see the World Series at home because it was on TV.

D. (Page 31)

In the first part of Exercise D, the correct order of the numbers is 2, 5, 4, 1, 3.

The correct order for the sentences is

1. Franklin D. Roosevelt had been president during World War II.
2. Harry S Truman was president at the end of the war.
3. The war was over, and many babies were born.
4. People could buy new cars again.
5. Twelve countries joined to form NATO.

E. (Page 31)

The blanks in the paragraph should be filled in as follows:

(1) in 1946, the *baby boom* began
(2) people began to use automatic machines in homes
(3) there were cars for people to buy
(4) baseball was on TV
(5) people were having fun

LESSON 9: INVENTIONS AND MODERN CONVENIENCES

A. (Page 32)

Students find and underline each sentence.

B. (Page 33)

1. Because of cars, more and better roads were built.
2. We use them to make life easier.
3. They could watch the news.
4. How would your life be without these three?
5. It took many years to invent the computer.
6. They make the air dirty.

C. (Page 33)

1. Cars got stuck because roads got muddy in the rain.
2. More roads were built because there were more cars.
3. Cars pollute the air because they burn gasoline.
4. Auto plants made new engines because they do not make the air as dirty.
5. People watched TV because they wanted information.
6. Computers are used at the Olympics because they make them run more smoothly.
7. People do math on computers because computers are faster.

D. (Page 34)

In the first part of Exercise D, the correct order of the numbers is 4, 2, 1, 5, 3.
The correct order of the sentences is

1. People began to buy cars.
2. Sometimes it rained on the dirt roads.
3. Then cars got stuck in the mud.
4. Good roads were built.
5. Now people who lived in the country could work in the city.

The blanks in the paragraph should be filled in as follows:

    (1) cars let us go where we want to go
    (2) TVs bring us the information we need
    (3) computers help do a lot of work quickly
    (4) We have more time to ride in our cars, watch TV, and use computers

LESSON 10: THE 1950S

A. (Page 36)
Students find and underline each sentence.

B. (Page 37)
1. She was arrested.
2. The Supreme Court said all students should go to school together.
3. Then they discarded them.
4. He knew war was terrible.
5. From there, it went into the rivers.
6. They bought many things.

C. (Page 37)
1. The water got dirty because chemicals got into it.
2. There is gasoline in the soil today because it leaked from underground tanks.
3. Eisenhower hated war because he had fought in World War II.
4. Parks didn't give her seat to a man because it was her seat.
5. The Supreme Court desegregated schools because it said all students should study together.

D. (Page 38)
In the first part of Exercise D, the correct order of the numbers is 1, 2, 3, 5, 4, 6.
    The correct order of the sentences is
1. In the 1950s, there was war, and there were some issues at home.
2. There was a war in Korea.
3. The United States sent troops.
4. At home, a Supreme Court decision desegregated the schools.
5. So life was fairer for some children.
6. Rosa Parks gave Americans a civil rights lesson.

E. (Page 38)
The blanks in the paragraph should be filled in as follows:

    (1) all schools were to serve all students
    (2) buses were no longer segregated
    (3) the fight for civil rights grew
    (4) life was a little fairer for some

LESSON 11: THE 1960S

A. (Page 39)
Students highlight or circle 18 words and phrases in the passage on page 39.

B. (Page 40)
I. John F. Kennedy
   president: 1961 to 1963
   1961
      Peace Corps
   César Chavez
   1962
      National Farm Workers Association

II. Lyndon B. Johnson
   president: 1963 to 1969
   1964
      Civil Rights Act
      "war on poverty"
   1967
      Thurgood Marshall
      Supreme Court

III. Neil Armstrong
   moon

C. (Page 41)
1. When was John F. Kennedy president?
2. When did César Chavez start the National Farm Workers Association?
3. When did the Peace Corps start?
4. When was Lyndon B. Johnson president?
5. When was the Civil Rights Act passed?
6. When did Thurgood Marshall join the Supreme Court?
7. When did Neil Armstrong walk on the moon?

D. (Page 41)
    (1) the Peace Corps began
    (2) the National Farm Workers Association began
    (3) the Civil Rights Act became law
    (4) President Johnson began a "war on poverty"
    (5) Thurgood Marshall was picked for the Supreme Court.
    (6) Neil Armstrong walked on the moon.

E. (Page 42)
Lyndon B. Johnson served as president from 1963 to 1969.
The Civil Rights Act was law in 1964.
He (Johnson) made a plan so people would not be poor.
When he was young, he himself had been poor.
His wish was for good health for older people.
He sent Thurgood Marshall to the Supreme Court in 1967.

LESSON 12: THE WAR IN VIETNAM

A. (Page 43)
Students highlight 16 words or phrases in the passage on page 43.

B. (Page 44)
I. Presidents Kennedy and Johnson
   early 1960s
   troops to Vietnam
      North Vietnam
      South Vietnam
   colleges
      protests
      marches

II. Richard M. Nixon
   president: 1969 to 1974
   1969
      Cambodia
      started to bomb
   1973
      troops left Vietnam

C. (Page 45)
1. Where was the United States at war in the 1960s?
2. Where were there protests and marches?
3. Where do many people from Cambodia, Laos, and Vietnam live today?
4. Where did people watch the war?
5. Where did the United States start to bomb in 1969?

D. (Page 45)
(1) Presidents Kennedy and Johnson sent troops there to fight
(2) people watched the war on TV
(3) students protested
(4) people marched
(5) the United States bombed Cambodia
(6) in 1973, U.S. troops came home

E. (Page 46)
1. Nixon served as president from 1969 to 1974.
2. The U.S. attacked Cambodia in 1969.
3. Then, in 1973, the United States pulled out of Vietnam.
4. The war was lost.
5. Many Americans are from Vietnam, Cambodia, and Laos.
6. They moved to the United States during the war in Vietnam or after the war was over.

LESSON 13: THE 1970S

A. (Page 47)
Students should highlight or circle 29 words and phrases in the passage on page 47.

B. (Page 48)
I. problem over oil
   dirty air and water
   polluted soil

II. Environmental Protection Agency
   1970
   helps
      people
      factories
   sets standards
   says what "clean" means

III. Gerald R. Ford
   president: 1974 to 1977
   1976
      bicentennial
      200 years old
   problem over oil
      comes from Arab nations
      stopped selling
      winter of 1976–77
         cold

IV. Jimmy Carter
   president: 1977
      Department of Energy

C. (Page 49)

1. What three environmental problems did the United States face in the 1970s?
2. What does EPA stand for?
3. What is the job of the EPA?
4. What problem did Ford face?
5. What countries supply a lot of oil?
6. What happened in the winter of 1976–77?
7. What department did President Carter form?

D. (Page 49)

(1) the air was dirty
(2) the water was dirty
(3) the soil was not clean, either
(4) the nation had to clean up the environment

E. (Page 50)

1. President Ford served from 1974 to 1977.
2. The United States had a big birthday party in 1976.
3. The nation was 200 years old.
4. Ford faced a problem with oil.
5. The Arab countries provide much oil to the world.
6. They were not selling it to the United States.
7. Americans had less oil to use.
8. People didn't keep their homes so warm.
9. There was a bad winter in 1976–1977.

LESSON 14: THE 1980S

A. (Page 51)

Students highlight 14 words and phrases in the passage on page 51.

B. (Page 52)

I. Ronald Reagan
    president: 1981 to 1989
    Sandra Day O'Connor
        Supreme Court
    1982
        cut taxes
    1980s
        computer use grew

II. George Bush
    president: 1989
        better schools
        cleaner environment
        no new taxes

C. (Page 53)

1. Who was president from 1981 to 1989?
2. Who was the first woman to serve on the Supreme Court?
3. Who gets tax money from people and businesses?
4. Who had more money after the tax cut?
5. Who wanted better schools and no new taxes?

D. (Page 53)

(1) Sandra Day O'Connor became the first woman to serve on the Supreme Court
(2) a lot of people were out of work in 1982
(3) President Reagan cut taxes
(4) fewer people were out of work in 1984
(5) In 1989, George Bush became president
(6) no new taxes

E. (Page 54)

1. Many people were out of work in 1982.
2. President Reagan lowered taxes.
3. Government took less money from companies.
4. Businesses kept more money.
5. This opened more jobs.
6. More people were back to work in 1984.

LESSON 15: THE 1990S

A. (Page 55)

Students highlight 17 words and phrases in the passage on page 55.

B. (Page 56)

I. *Technology*
    computers and computer connections
        communicate
        information

II. Bill Clinton
    elected president in 1992

III. Middle 1990s
    used computers more and more
    watched less TV
    Internet
        schools

IV. *North American Free Trade Agreement*
    Canada
    Mexico
    United States
        trade freely

C. (Page 57)

1. What made life move faster in the 1950s?
2. What made life move faster in the 1990s?
3. What got better between 1993 and 1997?
4. What did people do less by the middle 1990s?
5. What technology did schools get in the 1990s?
6. What does NAFTA stand for?
7. What countries signed NAFTA?
8. What do NAFTA countries do?

D. (Page 57)

(1) it made life go faster
(2) it helped people communicate
(3) it brought information to people everywhere
(4) Schools connected to the Internet
(5) the people all over the United States were using technology

E. (Page 58)

1. Canada, Mexico, and the United States signed the North American Free Trade Agreement in 1993.
2. These nations trade without tax.
3. All produce goods.
4. There are factories in each country.
5. NAFTA allows these factories free trade.
6. This way Mexico can buy more from the United States.
7. Canada can buy more too.

BUILDING SKILLS FOR SOCIAL STUDIES TOPIC INDEX